Tax Accounting

A Guide for Small Business Owners Wanting to Understand Tax Deductions, and Taxes Related to Payroll, LLCs, Self-Employment, S Corps, and C Corporations

Contents

Introduction

"In this world, nothing is certain except death and taxes." – Benjamin Franklin

Taxes are so important to where the great mafia gangster Al Capone was arrested not because of his many violent crimes but because of tax evasion. That is why with business, taxation is one of the most, if not the most important aspect areas.

For getting your business's taxes right, tax accounting is of utmost importance. Knowing how to do it properly enables you to get your financial records in order and, ultimately, ensure compliance with all tax regulations. Not only that, but it will also help you minimize your tax obligations and, consequently, maximize profitability.

In this book, you will learn all the important aspects of business taxation, such as:

- What tax accounting is
- Following government guidelines
- The difference between accounting and bookkeeping
- Payroll taxes and how to handle them
- Tax deductions
- Choosing the right business entity

More important, this book was written, keeping lay businesspeople like you in mind. Thus, it is written in a relatively simple and uncomplicated way. By the time you're done reading this book, you'll have all the information needed to manage your small business's taxes correctly and efficiently.

Let's get right into this important part of your business!

Chapter 1: What is Tax Accounting?

Tax accounting is a specific subsector of accounting that focuses more on – surprise, surprise – tax returns and payments instead of financial statement preparation. It is governed by the Internal Revenue Code of the IRS, which gives particular rules that individuals and businesses need to follow when preparing their tax returns.

Tax accounting is more particular about income, qualifying deductions, donations, and investment gains/losses for individuals. Tax accounting takes other things into consideration for businesses, making it much more complex compared to personal tax accounting. It places greater scrutiny on how they spend funds and identifying taxable and non-taxable transactions. Regardless if personal or for your business, tax accounting zeroes in on how you or your enterprise uses and receives funds.

Tax Accounting Vs. Financial Accounting

If you operate a business in the United States, you need to be familiar with two kinds of accounting principles: financial accounting and tax accounting. Don't make the mistake of confusing one for the other because you may get in trouble with the IRS if you do. To help you clearly distinguish one from the other, let's consider their key differences.

First, tax accounting is governed by the IRS' Internal Revenue Code, while financial accounting is based on generally accepted accounting principles or GAAP, under which businesses need to comply with common sets of accounting standards, principles, and procedures when recording financial transactions and preparing financial statements.

With GAAP, you may choose a specific method for recording financial transactions that impact the amount of taxes your business must pay. Let's use inventories as an example.

If you're operating a trading business, you have the option of using a FIFO (first-in, first-out) or LIFO (last in, first out) method for recording the cost of your sales. What do these mean?

With FIFO, you will use inventories that your business bought first as a basis for computing for gross profit. Let's say today, your business sold ten pairs of basketball shoes, and your beginning inventory consisted of 15 pairs that you purchased in two batches. The first batch consisted of seven pairs at $100 each, while the second batch consisted of eight pairs at $102 each. Your store sold each pair for $120.

Under the FIFO method, the cost of the first seven pairs sold is $100. This gives you a profit margin of $20 per pair for a total of $140. Since the $100 pairs were already sold, the next three sales were taken from the next batch bought at $102 each. The gross profit margin for each of the last three pairs sold for the day is $18, for a total of $54. Adding up the gross profits from all ten sales gives you

$194 in gross profits. Assuming all other expenses for the day amounted to $150, your business has a net taxable income of $44.

What if your business used LIFO instead? Using the same example, you will first get inventory from the most recent batch of purchases, i.e., the $102 pairs of shoes. Thus, the first eight pairs sold will be costed at $102 each for a gross profit of $18 for the first eight pairs sold today. The total for this is $144.

The remaining two pairs sold will come from the next most recent batch of inventory purchases, i.e., the $100 pairs. This gives your business a gross profit of $20 for each of the last two sales, totaling $40.

For the entire day, your store earned a total gross profit of $188, which is $6 less than using FIFO. With expenses still at $150, the net taxable income for the day is only $38.

Financial accounting covers all financial transactions of your business, from purchasing inventory to interest on bank deposits, but tax accounting only focuses on financial transactions that impact your tax liabilities. Given that the IRS regulates tax accounting in the United States, all income-earning individuals and registered businesses need to comply with it, both to pay the right amounts and filing the right forms. Failure to do so may cause serious penalties, charges, or even lawsuits.

If you're self-employed, a practicing professional, or operating a small/simple business, you have the option of doing tax accounting yourself. It's because chances are, your financial transactions are simple. But if you're operating a big business such as a corporation, financial transactions may be more complicated, and the complexity of business taxes requires hiring a professional tax accountant. Otherwise, you risk doing the taxes wrong and getting in trouble with tax authorities.

Individual Tax Accounting

If you're an individual taxpayer, all you need to focus on regarding tax accounting are income, qualifying deductions, and investment gains or losses. Given the limited information to manage and the simplicity of financial transactions for tax return purposes, hiring a tax accountant is optional, as you may do it yourself.

Business Tax Accounting

Depending on the nature, size, and complexity of the business, hiring a tax accountant may be necessary.

While the fund-tracking processes are the same for individuals earning income and for businesses, the latter may involve more complex uses of funds for specific expenses or liabilities. These may include particular types of business expenses that aren't applicable to individuals and payments to owners, especially corporate shareholders.

While businesses are not legally mandated to hire a tax accountant, it may be in your best interest to do so. By doing so, you can focus your time, energy, and resources on effectively managing and growing your business. And if your business is a corporation, a tax accountant may be considered a necessary hire due to the complexity of financial transactions, information, and records.

Tax-Exempt Organizations

It may sound odd, but yes, even these types of organizations need tax accounting. Why?

Most organizations are required by the IRS to submit annual returns, i.e., information on total grants, donations, and other similar fund inflows and how they use the funds they receive. While they're not required to pay income taxes, they need to show proof they are continuously complying with all requirements for tax-exempt entities.

Why Tax Accounting is Important to Your Business

The most important reason for tax accounting is because you are legally obliged to file and pay the right amount of taxes on your income. If you don't, you and/or your business can get into a lot of trouble. Think of it this way: one of American history's most powerful and evasive crime lords – Al Capone – wasn't arrested for murders and gang-related stuff but because of tax evasion. Think about that!

From a profitability standpoint, you can also maximize the return on your investment in a business with proper tax accounting knowledge. A good example is deciding whether to borrow money or put in more capital into an existing business.

There are two ways to increase your business funding: investing more equity capital or borrowing money with interest. On the surface, it seems that investing more capital is the more sensible thing to do, considering that borrowing money will require paying interest. This can obviously affect the amount of expected net income.

But if you are familiar with the concept of return on investment and how tax accounting rules apply, you're probably thinking that depending on the loan and the expected revenue increase, there's always the chance that borrowing money - even at interest - may be the more profitable option.

Allow me to illustrate with a specific example. Let's say your hardware business has the opportunity to earn an additional $5000 in revenue by investing $10,000 in new equipment. Let's assume that you will need extra funds in the same amount to be able to buy said equipment.

Let us also assume these figures:

- Current annual revenue averages $100,000
- Current average annual expenses total $85,000

- The expected increase in annual revenues from the purchase of equipment = $5,000

- The interest rate on borrowed money is at 5% p.a.

- The tax rate is 30%

The first option is to invest more money in the business, $10,000 to be more specific. If you have an equity balance of $50,000 in your existing business, doing this raises your equity or total investment to $60,000.

By putting in $10,000 of additional equity, you can buy the equipment and expect annual revenues to increase to $105,000. Assuming no increase in average annual expenses, expected net income before taxes can go up to $20,000. Assuming a tax rate of 30%, the expected net income after tax would be $14,000. To get the expected return on equity investment, just divide the expected after-tax income buy the $60,000 equity balance, and you will get an ROI of 23.33%

Now, let's consider the second option: borrow money at 5% interest per annum. Borrowing $10,000 at this rate will cause interest expenses totaling $500, assuming a lump sum payment at the end of the loan. This means average annual expenses may go up to $85,500.

Given the expected increase in revenues to $105,000 because of the equipment purchase, your business is expected net income before tax will be $19,500 only, which is slightly lower compared to that of infusing an additional $10,000 in the capital. With a 30% tax rate, the expected after-tax net income will be around $13,650, which is still slightly lower compared to option number one.

It may be tempting to think that it's simply better to invest the additional $10,000 into the business. You may have to forego on other important things so you can increase your business's after-tax income by an additional $4,000 annually.

This is where the concept of return on investment comes into play. This metric shows you if it is worth putting in extra money in your business or to borrow money at cost. To get the expected return on equity investment for the first option, which is to put in more money, divide the expected after-tax income for that option by $60,000. This is the new equity balance after you put in the additional $10,000. So, $14,000 / 60,000 dollars will give you an ROI of 23.33%.

Now, let's consider the ROI for the second option, which is to borrow $10,000 to buy that new equipment at an interest rate of 5% annually. The expected after-tax profit for this option is $13,650. Because you borrowed money instead of investing your own $10,000 into the business, your equity balance will remain at $50,000 only. Doing the same thing as we did with the first option, you will get an ROI of 27.30% when you divide the expected net income after tax over your business is equity balance.

What is the implication of this? under these conditions, you'll get more bang for your buck by just borrowing money at 5% annual interest instead of committing $10,000 of your own money to increase average annual revenues by $5000. You can use that $10,000 for other important things in your life or other more profitable investments. And without basic knowledge of tax accounting rules, you cannot analyze these two options from this perspective.

Hiring a Tax Accountant

Depending on your business's nature and size, tax return preparations can be simple enough to DIY or may need the services of a professional tax accountant. But regardless if yours is small and simple or a large and complex type, hiring a tax expert to do your business's tax accounting is the safest way to go. It's because doing so can help you focus on higher-level responsibilities and tasks such as growing your business and looking for new customers or clients.

Another benefit of hiring a tax accountant to do the process for your business is expertise. Doing so minimizes your risks for tax-related violations, intentional or not, and maximizes your chances of coming up with the best tax strategy for the long term.

And speaking of planning your business's taxes, most of your business decisions are likely to have tax-related effects. That is why even if you currently operate a small and simple business, hiring a tax accountant can help you grow your business and make good business decisions that can minimize future taxes and maximize long term income.

If you have the budget for it and hire one, how do you make sure that you hire a good tax accountant? Here are the characteristics you need to consider on the shortlist and eventually choose the person.

Internal Revenue Code Knowledge

The Internal Revenue Code is the basis for all tax accounting rules in the United States. It gives taxpayers guidelines on how to account for income changes on their corporate or individual tax returns. It is your Bible for all things pertaining to taxes.

A very knowledgeable tax accountant isn't just one familiar with the code from years ago, but it's also one constantly up to date with changes in the regulatory framework. The IRS frequently changes the Internal Revenue Code, on top of new laws with a significant impact on United States taxes. In the last 10 years alone, the IRS has an estimated over 3,250 tax code changes. Hence, you have to ensure that the tax accountant you choose is regularly updating their tax code knowledge.

Given the number of changes in the last 10 years alone, can you imagine ensuring your business's *perfect compliance* with tax accounting rules? While it's highly unlikely that all these changes affect your small or medium-sized business, you will still need to be updated because you'll never know if changes can significantly affect your business. Now, can you see the value of hiring a tax accountant?

Financial Accounting Expertise

Although tax accounting rules differ from financial accounting ones, your tax accountant still needs to be highly knowledgeable in financial accounting. Why? Without such a foundation, it's difficult to record proper balances for more peculiar accounts, such as deferred tax assets and for deferred tax liabilities. If you remember the discussion earlier on deferred tax liabilities, only a person familiar with both tax accounting and financial accounting rules can properly record balances for it because it results from differences in the two.

General Entrepreneurial Knowledge

Many entrepreneurs and companies prefer working with tax accountants who don't just know how to file tax returns but can also help them with strategizing their business. Because most – if not all – business decisions ultimately affect taxes, tax accountants who are also adept at business and financial planning are very in demand.

Choosing one who is also well-versed with a good, holistic view of business will greatly benefit your business. More than just the ability to help you minimize taxes and maximize returns on your investment, he or she can also help you run your business much better.

Licensed

While tax accountants need not be licensed CPAs, choosing one with a license should be your priority. When your tax accountant is licensed, he or she understands the relationship between financial and tax accounting, which is key to helping you ensure compliance and minimize taxes for your business.

Chapter 2: Following Tax Guidelines

Now that you have a clear idea of what tax accounting is and how it's different from financial accounting, you need to be familiar with basic tax guidelines. After all, the primary goal of tax accounting is to ensure proper compliance with tax regulations, i.e., filing the right kinds and amounts of taxes, and doing so on time. Here are the most important things you must know about tax accounting for your business as a business owner.

Hobby or Business

Are you into hobbies that also double as sources of extra income like baking, video editing, or songwriting? While all income sources are subject to tax return requirements, there are different rules for reporting income from hobbies and from businesses. If a side business involves a favorite hobby, consider these tips for taking advantage of special limits and rules for tax deductions on the income.

Tip #1: Determine If It's a Business or Hobby

One of the key characteristics of businesses is that they're profit-oriented (obviously). In contrast, you engage in hobbies and interests for the sheer pleasure of it. Income, if any, is just a by-product.

To help you objectively determine whether what you're doing is a business or a hobby for taxation purposes, the IRS recommends considering the following factors:

- Whether you carry on the activity in a businesslike manner and maintain complete and accurate books and records

- Whether the time and effort you put into the activity indicates you intend to make it profitable

- Whether you depend on income from the activity for your livelihood

- Whether your losses are due to circumstances beyond your control or are normal in the startup phase for your business type

- Whether you change your methods of operation in an attempt to improve profitability

- Whether you or your advisors have the knowledge needed to carry on the activity as a successful business

- Whether you succeeded in making a profit in similar activities in the past

- Whether the activity makes a profit in a few years and how much profit it makes

- Whether you can expect to make a future profit from the appreciation of the assets used in the activity

Tip #2: Know the Allowed Hobby-Related Deductions

As a taxpayer, you can – within specific limits – deduct ordinary and necessary expenses related to your hobbies for tax return purposes. Ordinary expenses are those that are par for the activity, i.e., accepted and common. Necessary expenses are those that apply to the hobby.

Let's say you're a handyman and making furniture is one of your hobbies. Examples of ordinary and necessary expenses are raw materials such as wood, nails, and paint, among others.

Tip #3: Learn the Limits on Hobby-Related Deductions

To maximize tax deductions from hobby-related activities, you must know the limits. The maximum amount of tax deductions you can enjoy from hobbies is the income associated with such activities. Unlike with business losses, i.e., when operating expenses exceed revenues or income, losses from hobbies can't be used as tax deductions for other income.

Tip #4: Know How to Deduct Expenses Related to Your Hobby

More than just knowing what and how much to deduct, you must also know how to do it properly. In general, you'll need to itemize all hobby-related deductions on your tax return, which may fall into one of three kinds of deductions, each having special rules. IRS' Publication 535 provides clear instructions on how to do it.

The Employer Identification Number (EIN)

Also called Federal Tax Identification, the EIN is used to identify business entities. Generally, businesses need to have it to operate.

How can you apply for your business's EIN? There are several ways to do so, including applying online. Regardless of your chosen method, remember that registering for one is free, and you can immediately get it upon application. Also, check with your state if your business needs to have a charter or a state number, too.

Online Application

For many entrepreneurs, online EIN applications are their preferred method. If you choose this method, too, you can get your business's EIN immediately once you've completed the application process, and the information you submitted has been validated. This process is available only for businesses with principal businesses, agencies, offices, or legal residences in the United States or any of its territories.

Facsimile Applications

If you still have a fax machine and would like to apply for an EIN using it, just fill up a Form SS-4 completely and fax it to the proper number. After the responsible office determines your business needs a new EIN, it will assign one to it via the applicable procedures for its type. If you provide your business's fax number, you can expect the EIN to be faxed within four business days.

Snail Mail Applications

If you mail in your business's EIN application, it will take you about 4 weeks, give or take. As with other modes, properly and completely fill up the Form SS-4 with the required information. If the responsible office determines your business requires a new EIN, it will assign one based on the business type and mail it to you. To find out where to mail your Form SS-4 based on your business's location, you can go to the following website.

https://www.irs.gov/filing/where-to-file-your-taxes-for-form-ss-4

Business Taxes

Your business structure will determine what kinds of taxes your enterprise will pay and how you do it. The five general kinds of business taxes are income, estimated, self-employment, employment, and excise taxes.

Income Taxes

Except for partnerships, all businesses need to file annual income tax returns. If your business is a partnership, it will have to file only an information return. We will talk about the specific forms you must use for your business in the succeeding chapters.

Federal income taxes are pay-as-you-go taxes, i.e., you or your business pays income taxes earned or received during the year. Employers normally withhold taxes from their employees' salaries. As a business, chances are your income tax isn't withheld or, if ever, what's withheld isn't sufficient such that you may need to pay estimated taxes. But if you or your business need not make estimated tax payments, you can simply pay the taxes due upon filing of income tax returns. More information on this is available here.

Estimated Taxes

As an entrepreneur, you will probably need to pay income taxes, including self-employment, via regular payments of estimated taxes. How do you know if you need to pay them?

If you're a sole proprietor, partnership, or an S corporation member or shareholder, you will need to make estimated tax payments if you strongly believe that your taxes for the year will be at least $1,000 upon filing. If your business is a corporation, that will likely owe at least $500 in income taxes by the time it files its tax returns. Also, you or your business will probably have to pay estimated taxes if taxes in the previous year were higher than $0.00.

To determine your business's estimated taxes, use Form 1040-ES. In doing so, you must estimate your adjusted gross income, taxable income, taxes, deductions, and tax credits for the current taxable year.

One way to get a fair estimate of the abovementioned items is by using information from the most recent taxable year as a starting point or average figures for the last several years' federal tax returns.

If you believe your estimated earnings are excessive, just complete another copy of Form 1040-ES so you can re-estimate next quarter's taxes. If your re-estimation is too low, repeat the process by filling up another copy of the form to recalculate next quarter's estimated taxes. Always remember that the more accurate your computations are, the higher your chances of avoiding penalties.

- Estimated taxes are filed and paid every quarter. You can send your estimated tax payments using Form 1040-ES via:

- Snail mail

- Online

- By phone

- Using the IRS2Go app

Of all the ways you can pay Federal taxes, the EFTPS or Electronic Federal Tax Payment System is the easiest to use. Through it, you can pay for all Federal taxes, including:

- FTDs or Federal tax deposits

- Installment tax payments

- Estimated tax payments

You even have the option to pay more often if it's easier for you or your business. You can do it weekly, every 2 weeks, monthly, every 2 months, etc. The only requirement is that your total estimated tax payments are enough by the end of the taxable quarter concerned.

Another significant benefit of paying taxes using this platform is access to payment history. Whenever you need to check past payment details, it's easy to extract records and get the information you need.

Self-Employment Taxes

Also called *SE taxes*, these refer to employment-related taxes for individuals or solopreneurs working for themselves. These contribute to your medical and social security coverage, including retirement, disability, hospitalization, and survivorship benefits.

You must pay self-employment taxes and file them using Forms 1040 or 1040-SR under any of these conditions:

- Your self-employment earnings total at least $400

- You received at least $108.28 in wages from a church or a qualified church-controlled organization that elected to be exempted from Medicare and social security taxes

Employment Taxes

If your business employs people, you have employment tax responsibilities to fulfill. In particular, you withhold, file, and pay your employees' taxes on the salaries and wages, you pay them. These include:

- Medicare

- Social security

- Federal income withholding taxes

- Federal unemployment taxes (FUTA)

Excise Taxes

These are specific to the sale or manufacturing of specific products, operating specific types of businesses, rendering particular kinds of services, and using different products, facilities, or equipment. These taxes, which require filling out specific forms, include:

- Accepting or conducting wagers or lottery draws

- Air transportation

- Communications

- Environmental

- Fuel

- Retail sales of heavy equipment

- Sales or use of specific products or articles

- Use of heavy vehicles on public highways

Record Keeping Guidelines

Ensuring good record keeping for tax and financial accounting purposes has a myriad number of benefits. These include:

- The ability to monitor your business's progress or digress accurately
- Accurate financial statements
- Clear identification of income sources
- Keeping track of tax-deductible expenses
- Accurate and timely payment and filing of tax returns

Given the many kinds of documents and financial records your business uses and creates in its operations, which of them should you keep? While the IRS doesn't require special types of records for businesses, the type of business you own will determine the kinds of records that require keeping. But in general, these include bank statements, official receipts issued and obtained, and invoices, among others. For tax accounting purposes, all financial documents evidencing income and expenses need to be retained.

For how long should you keep records? Ideally, for long. It's because you'll never know when you'll need to show proof for specific transactions and/or claims, but if resource constraints prevent you from keeping all documents from day one, consider the IRS' prescriptions (from their website) for how long you should keep records for income tax purposes:

1. Three years if situations (4), (5), and (6) below do not apply to you

2. Three years from the when the original return was filed, or two years from the when the tax was paid, whichever comes last if you file a claim for credit or refund after you file your return

3. Seven years if you file a claim about losses arising from writing off bad-debts or worthless financial securities

4. Six years if you do not report income you were supposed to, and it's above 25% of the gross income reported on the return

5. Indefinitely if you do not file a return

6. Indefinitely if you file a fraudulent return

7. Keep employment tax records for at least four years after the date that the tax becomes due or is paid, whichever is later

For your employees' withholding taxes, you must keep at records for the last four years at the minimum.

When you file your or your business's tax returns, you're responsible for proving the authenticity of all information in them, such as entries, deductions, and statements. Often called the burden of proof. If your business practices excellent record-keeping, substantiating information in your tax returns will not be problematic or stressful.

The Tax Year

When filing tax returns, you need to determine your taxable income within the taxable or tax year. This refers to the annual accounting period for record-keeping and income/expense reporting to the IRS. Remember that a yearly accounting period excludes short tax years.

You have two options for determining your business's tax year. These are calendar and fiscal. When you choose a calendar tax year or calendar year, your business's annual accounting period begins every 1st of January and culminates at the end of December 31. If you choose a fiscal year, the tax year is 12 consecutive months ending on the final day of the 12th month, except for December. It can be from February 1 to January 31 of the following year or from June 1 to May 31 of the next year.

By default, your business adopts a tax year when you fill out its first income tax return based on that tax year, but a specific tax year is sometimes required, in which case, it's the default one. A required tax year is one that the IRS and tax regulations require.

Many taxpayers mistakenly think they have specifically adopted a tax year while they haven't. Don't make the same mistake. Doing the following doesn't mean you have adopted a tax year for your business:

- Applying to extend the deadline for income tax return filing

- Submitting an employer identification number (EIN)

- Paying estimated taxes for the current tax year.

Once you file your business's initial tax return using a calendar year, there are only two ways to change to a fiscal year. The first is with express IRS approval and the second is if your enterprise meets specific exceptions found in Form 1128, i.e., Application to Adopt, Change, or Retain a Tax Year.

Usually, any business can adopt either a calendar or a fiscal tax year. The calendar year is your only option if:

- Your business neither keeps records nor maintains accounting books

- It has no annual accounting period

- The business's current tax year doesn't qualify as fiscal

- Income tax regulations of the Internal Revenue Code specifically mandates your business to use a calendar year

Short Tax Years

This refers to those that are less than 12 months, which the IRS may require when your business - as a taxable entity - has:

- Existed for less than a full tax year

- Changed its accounting period

In the first scenario where your business hasn't existed for 12 consecutive months yet, it still needs to file a tax return for the number of months it had earned income. Fortunately, the tax-filing requirements and tax determination process are the same as for full ones, i.e., 12 months, that end on the last day of short tax years. If you want more information on this, check out the IRS' Publication 538 on Accounting Periods and Methods.

If you decide to change your business's accounting period at a later time, you will need approval from the IRS to do so, using its Form 1128, i.e., Application to Adopt, Change, or Retain a Tax Year. Unless your application qualifies for automatic approval, an IRS ruling in favor of the tax year change and payment of a user fee is required.

Tax Audits

As a small business owner, you'll be very hands on in managing your enterprise. You may be consumed with high-level functions like:

- Acquiring new clients or expanding market share
- Business innovations
- Customer service
- Hiring staff
- Strategizing
- Making money

Not only are record-keeping and tax accounting tedious and time-consuming, but they also don't contribute to the bottom-line. Hence, the chances are that you will put much less consideration for these. This can put you at risk during tax audits because of possible tax computing mistakes. Many entrepreneurs, especially small business owners, consider tax audits bad news. It also doesn't help that audits, regardless if conducted by the IRS or an external auditor, can disrupt normal operations.

Now that you're aware of these, make avoiding tax audits one of your business's top priorities. While it can't totally avoid getting audited, understanding the most common IRS red flags for tax audits and avoiding them can help your business minimize the chances of catching the IRS attention. Here are those red flags that you should avoid as much as possible:

1. Multiple and/or Consecutive Net Annual Losses

If your business reported net losses for three out of the last five tax years, the IRS would likely give it a friendly visit. Those chances are even higher if yours is a sole proprietorship because of the tendency to co-mingle personal and business funds. Hence, prepare for a tax audit if these happen.

One of the best ways to minimize the risk of incurring at least three years of net losses in five years is to review your business' revenues and deductions, making sure they're accurate and reasonable. You may need to forego deductions if only to avoid red flagging your business to the IRS with more than two unprofitable years out of five.

2. Habitually Late Filing of Returns

Submitting your business' tax returns past the deadline isn't just costly. It also draws the IRS' attention and increases the likelihood of a tax audit. So, ensuring the timely filing of tax returns doesn't just save you money but also minimizes tax audit risks. This is one area where procrastination shouldn't be tolerated, not even a whiff.

3. Excessive Salaries

If your business offers shares of the company to employees, you'll need to be cautious about giving them reasonable salaries. Why? Simply put, company shareholders also earning large salaries from the company draw the IRS like flowers attract bees.

This will not likely be the most serious issue your business may face if tax audited. Chances are that the bigger concern would be if the enterprise continues to rake in more money with each passing year.

To minimize this risk, make sure you have a good grasp of the average salary for employees in your industry. That way, you can structure salaries competitively but not excessively. This can help you avoid being on the IRS' tax audit radar.

4. Countless Number of Deductions

While deductions are important for minimizing your business's taxes, you need to use them wisely. Not every expense qualifies as legitimate deductions for business purposes. If you have the habit of charging just about every expense under the sun as deductions, you increase the likelihood of drawing the IRS's attention. This is especially true if you're operating a sole proprietorship. Worse, once the IRS discovers your business's excessive and unqualified deductions, it may impose penalties.

To avoid getting flagged for too many deductions, review your business's deductions for the last few years for consistency. But if you just started a new business, better to check with an accountant to ensure you only charge ordinary and necessary expenses as deductions for your business per IRS guidance.

5. Large Donations to Charities

While giving such can be a very noble endeavor, it's better to err on the side of caution by keeping the amounts moderate or low. Why?

Giving huge sums of money to charity often gives the IRS the impression that a business is up to something. It's because many businesses use charitable donations as a way to avoid taxes. The IRS considers this as a blatant abuse of the internal revenue code, which can severely punish.

Make it a win-win situation for your business and its benefactors by giving reasonable donations consistently every year, regardless of how high or low its earnings are. This gives the practice a semblance of normalcy, which is crucial for avoiding the IRS' radar and, consequently, tax audits.

6. Excessive Use of the Business' Vehicle

Especially for a sole proprietorship, claiming full business use of your vehicle puts the business at high risk for catching the eye of tax authorities and inviting them to conduct a tax audit. When deducting a vehicle's business use for tax purposes, you have the option of using the actual amount of expense, the IRS standard mileage rate, or both throughout a tax year, but using them both when filing tax returns is a glaring red flag for the IRS. Claiming 100% business use for depreciating a vehicle also requires documentary evidence for every trip the car was used for.

To minimize your business's risks for being red-flagged by the IRS for excessive business use of vehicles, it's crucial that you carefully consider how they're used and ensure only the actual business-related uses are claimed for tax-filing purposes. Only the following may be valid business-related uses of vehicles:

- Going to client meetings
- Traveling to conduct research
- Posting mail for the business
- Any other activities directly related to your business

Clearly, using the car to go for a gym workout or drive your spouse to work isn't justifiable business-related vehicle uses.

7. Transacting in Cash

Believe it or not, but if your business deals mostly in cash, its chances of catching the eye of tax authorities are much higher. Why? It's because verifying income earned in cash can be way harder compared to non-cash transactions. Also, large purchases (equipment, vehicles, properties, etc.) using cash isn't par for the course and usually causes concern. Why not pay in check or via credit card, both of which are far safer and more practical than lugging around a ton of cash? Those that do so are usually trying to hide something and usually what they're trying to hide is illegal.

To avoid getting red-flagged because of this, use a cheque, credit, or debit card for high-ticket purchases. But if you're more comfortable using cash or if transactions require it, just ensure high-precision and details in recording them and establish clear paper trails through documents like official receipts, invoices, etc. And for single buyer receipts for amounts greater than $10,000 within a 12-month period, make sure to fill out Form 8300 completely.

8. Rounded Numbers and Erroneous Calculations

One of the most common problems small business owners face when they do their own tax returns results from using numbers rounded off instead of exact figures. This practice often results in erroneous tax return calculations, which can be a red flag for the IRS to do a tax audit.

To minimize your business's risks for being flagged due to wrongly calculated tax figures, avoid using averages or rounding off numbers to the nearest dollar. Instead, always use decimal points when calculating earnings and expenses for tax return filing purposes.

9. Use Schedule C Filings Carefully

As a sole proprietor, you will need to use schedule C form 1040 to calculate your business's Tax deductions. These may include expenses such as interest paid on loans, advertising, and Home Office deductions.

Why should you be very careful when using this form? Many experts think this increases the likelihood of being audited by the IRS. But this doesn't mean you should avoid it altogether. It shouldn't have to be a choice between getting tax audited or weaving your rights to tax deductions, especially those that are legitimate and valid. Just be very careful about the deductions you will claim, both in kind and in amount, to avoid catching the unwanted attention of tax authorities.

If it's your first time to get into business or if you're not yet that familiar with tax accounting, it's best to seek professional advice. That is why I can never overemphasize the benefit of letting a professional tax accountant do the work for your business.

10. Not Reporting Taxable Income

If ever there's such a thing as a mortal sin to the Internal Revenue Service, that would be a failure to report all of your business's taxable income. Especially for small business owners like you, tax authorities expect reporting all income earned within the United States, which includes income kept in offshore accounts, payments received in cash, and other kinds of income. You can be sure that the IRS will come knocking at your business's door to conduct a tax audit if they see you fail to report all of your business's taxable income.

As a small business owner, especially if you're a sole proprietor, it's important for you to maintain well organized and kept records and to avoid commingling of personal and business assets and liabilities. Doing so ensures you avoid non-reporting of taxable income, even if unintentional. Remember, the IRS doesn't distinguish between erroneous and intentional under-reporting of taxable income. They will still penalize infractions the same way.

11. Claiming Losses on Rentals

Under certain conditions, claiming losses from rentals in real estate businesses are allowed, but doing this isn't as easy or simple as it sounds. For one, claiming such losses is the same as wearing a luminous neon shirt while running in the dark. It makes your business even more visible to the tax authorities and increases its chances of being subjected to a tax audit. If you want to take advantage of actual rental losses by claiming them in your business's tax returns, let a seasoned tax accountant do it. Doing so minimizes the chances of erroneous computations, and if ever your business is audited, it will not be considered a finding.

12. Excluding Foreign-Earned Income

This would only apply to you if you are a small business owner that either works out of the country for a significant portion of a tax year, you make money overseas, or both. If this is you, you can be eligible to claim exclusions on the income you earn abroad, but having very strict and rigid requirements for claiming these will most likely catch the attention of the IRS and subject you to a tax audit. So, consult with a tax accountant who has experience with such exclusions to minimize your risks.

13. Using Cryptocurrencies

Because cryptocurrencies such as Ethereum and Bitcoin are relatively new financial assets and are considered autonomous from any Regulatory agency, using them in your business can make the IRS interested and conduct an audit. Being beyond regulating governments, these are often used for funding criminal activities. The best thing you can do with cryptocurrencies is to limit them to your personal use. That way, you won't tick off tax authorities.

During Tax Audits

As soon as the IRS notifies you of an impending tax audit, contact your accountant right away. If you don't have one by the time a tax audit is due, I highly recommend hiring a tax accountant as soon as possible. Preferably, he or she must be on board by the time tax authorities conduct the audit.

• There are other things you can do to get through tax audits with minimal stress and complications. These include:

• Keep a positive attitude. This is even more important during your interactions with IRS agents. To make the entire audit process move smoothly and quickly, always be courteous and honest when dealing with them.

• Make sure your financial records are well organized. By doing this, it will be easy for you to present supporting documents for the transactions IRS agents may look into. When your records are in disarray, presenting valuable documents may become difficult and give agents the impression that something is up, even when things are normal.

• Always be clear and honest. With your accountant, always strive to present all required documents so you can clearly and honestly support your income tax computations to the auditors.

• Read all IRS notices. Ignoring them will neither prevent an audit from happening nor get you through one once it starts.

As a small business owner, preparing taxes is already challenging. Can you imagine the added stress of being audited by the IRS, too? If your business gets tax audited, be ready for a comprehensive and sometimes extended process. It's because tax authorities will probably ask you lots of questions and ask for many documents to show your reported income and deductions' accuracy and legitimacy.

Being aware of the misconceptions regarding tax audits can also help you prepare for them well. Some of these include:

• Low-income taxpayers don't get audited. Small businesses and sole proprietors can also be subject to tax audits regardless of how big or small their incomes are.

• The time frame covered by tax audits is limited to just one year. If you think this is the case, you're in big trouble. The Internal Revenue Service has up to three years to audit the tax returns you filed for your business. So, don't be complacent, thinking you will no longer be audited just because the tax season is over.

• Your business's tax returns can be audit proofed. Yes, the red flag tips presented above can help minimize the chances of your business being tax audited, but that does not mean you are guaranteed to escape tax audits. All taxpayers are eligible to be tax audited, and the best thing that can happen is to minimize the chances of winning this tax lottery.

Chapter 3: Learning Accounting and Bookkeeping

Before proceeding any further, you will need to distinguish bookkeeping from accounting. While both are necessary for your business, they have key differences you will need to know. They may have the same goals for starters, but they provide different types of support throughout your business's financial cycles.

Between the two, bookkeeping is more administrative and transactional. It focuses more on the proper and consistent recording of financial transactions for a business. Accounting may be considered the more subjective endeavor between the two. It is because, at its core, accounting provides business owners like you with important business insights such as the financial health and performance of your enterprise using information curated through bookkeeping.

Bookkeeping

This process focuses primarily on recording all financial transactions in consistent ways compliant with generally accepted accounting principles or GAAP. the main components of bookkeeping include:

- Recording of financial transactions
- Debit and credit postings
- Issuing invoices
- Creating, maintaining, and balancing of ledgers (both subsidiary and general) and historical accounts
- Managing payroll

General Ledger maintenance is one of the key aspects of bookkeeping. General ledgers are basic documents on which a bookkeeper records financial transactions such as revenues and expenses. This activity is normally called posting, and with more sales and other financial transactions, the more postings a Ledger receives. For your business, you or your bookkeeper can create ledgers using specialized software, a basic computer spreadsheet such as Excel or Numbers, or even a simple lined sheet of paper.

How complex should your bookkeeping system be? Well, it would depend on your business's size, the number of transactions, and how often they happen. All sales revenues and purchases are recorded directly in the Ledger, and certain items require supporting documents. The IRS clarifies which business transactions need to be supported by these.

Accounting

Accounting is a high-level activity that makes use of the information collected through bookkeeping to create financial documents, models, and analysis that reflect a business's financial condition and performance. Accounting is more subjective compared to bookkeeping because the latter is more transactional. The main components of accounting include:

- Preparation of adjusting entries

- Preparing financial statements

- Analysis of a business's operations, including costs and revenues

- Preparation and filing of income tax returns

- Helping owners like you understand the potential effects of making key financial decisions for the business

One reason why accounting is important is that it can give you reports that use financial indicators to give you a clear picture of your business's financial health and performance. Is your business making money consistently? Is it growing? Is it strong enough to withstand black Swans or unforeseen economic events? Does it have enough funds to meet all of its financial obligations? These are a few of the most important questions accounting can help you answer so you can make the best financial decisions possible for your enterprise.

That is why when it comes to seeking advice and counsel on key business issues, your accountant is one of your best friends. Using the information available through bookkeeping, he or she can help you manage your business profitably, make sure you pay the right taxes on time, and make fairly reliable financial forecasts.

The Bookkeeper Vs. the Accountant

Because they have the same goal in helping your business, sometimes, a bookkeeper and accountant do the same work. But usually the first task of a bookkeeper is to record your business's financial transactions and to make sure its finances and books are in order. But an accountant will mostly focus on consultation, advice, and analysis of your business's financial performance and health, and managing its taxes optimally.

What are a few of the credential's bookkeepers need to have? Normally, they need not have a formal education to practice bookkeeping, but a business or accounting educational and professional background is ideal. This is to make sure that they understand how business works to record financial transactions properly.

One indispensable characteristic a bookkeeper must have is strict attention to detail. It is because he or she will be responsible for recording all financial transactions of the business. If careless, it is easy to record the wrong amount which may significantly affect the accuracy of financial statements and tax returns.

Normally, an accountant supervises the bookkeeper. Sometimes, you as the business owner, do it. And because accountants need to be certified to render services for clients, bookkeepers can't be called accountants.

For a person to be qualified as an accountant, he or she needs to have a bachelor's degree in accounting. If not, a degree in finance can be an adequate substitute. And unlike bookkeepers, accountants need to be certified. Having the title of a certified public accountant or CPA may be considered a reliable seal or indicator of professionalism and expertise. To have this designation, a person must pass the Unified Certified Public Accountant Examination and must have enough experience in the industry of professional accounting.

To give you a clear picture of the key differences between bookkeeping and accounting, check out the table below:

Bookkeeping	Accounting
Involves recording and categorizing a business's financial transactions.	Involves preparation of adjusting book entries.
Posting of debits and credits.	Financial statement preparation.
Preparation and issuance of invoices.	Preparation and filing of income tax returns.
Maintenance and balancing of the subsidiary and general ledgers, and historical accounts of the business.	Conducting financial analysis based on information collected through bookkeeping and formulating strategies.
Payroll management.	Tax planning and strategizing.
Record-keeping.	Financial forecasting.

To cap off the comparison between accounting and bookkeeping, both are important for your business's success and longevity. Bookkeeping ensures your business has accurate, complete, and organized financial records with properly balanced finance. But accounting helps you create smart financial strategies for growing and keeping your business profitable and making sure that it files the right taxes on time.

Many business owners prefer to learn how to manage their businesses' finances themselves. Others prefer hiring bookkeepers and accountants so they can focus on the more important aspects of running their businesses. This now begs the question: should you do your business's bookkeeping or hire somebody else to do it?

Bookkeeping for Your Business: DIY or Delegate

As a small business owner, one of the business decisions you must make regularly is whether to do something yourself or hire somebody else to do it for you. Each option has its own set of costs and benefits. That is why there is no single best answer. You will need to consider your business-like finances, performance, and nuances.

Doing It Yourself

While it's true that hiring a bookkeeper is the most convenient option, it may not necessarily be the right one for your business. You see, you'll need to consider several factors relevant to your business, such as its size, complexity of operations, and the number of transactions regularly. It's possible that daily bookkeeping for your small business is simple enough to do yourself. Transactions that you must consider include creating and sending invoices, monitoring expenses, recording payments and revenues, and managing taxes.

Getting the services of a bookkeeper entails costs. On average, hiring a bookkeeper can set you back $500-$2500 a month based on the complexity, size of business and number of transactions. If your business is small and your finances are very simple to handle by yourself, outsourcing both may not be a practical option for your business. The payoffs associated with hiring someone to do bookkeeping for you may be minimal to its cost.

Also, if your business services clients and builds them every month only, then the number of business transactions may also be moderate or even minimal. It may also not make sense to hire a bookkeeper because the amount of time you need to commit to bookkeeping may be minimal.

Under these two scenarios, doing the bookkeeping for your business by yourself may be the rational option.

One of the benefits of doing the bookkeeping yourself is getting deep insights regarding your business's actual health and performance. Instead of depending on bank statements to determine your business's profitability and sustainability, DIY bookkeeping keeps you abreast of all important aspects of the business, such as revenues, expenses, and average collection periods.

This isn't the only benefit associated with doing your business' bookkeeping. Being on top of your enterprise's finances helps you discover and nip cash flow problems in the bud, identify major fluctuations in revenues and income, and make more informed and objective financial decisions for your business.

If you feel you're going way over your head by trying to assume your business's bookkeeping responsibilities, don't worry. There are many resources to help you learn the basics of bookkeeping and even accounting. And if you plan to use or are already using reliable accounting software, the developer probably also provides free user training.

Outsourcing

The primary advantage or benefit of outsourcing bookkeeping responsibilities is convenience. You can free up a lot of time you can use to focus on other important areas to grow your business. As a small business owner, the amount of time you can free up by hiring a bookkeeper can be very valuable as you take on the many heavy responsibilities associated with entrepreneurship, especially if you think you are already spread too thin.

Ask your business grows, the volume and complexity of financial transactions increase. It may come to where you can no longer do the bookkeeping functions yourself, or at least do it well enough. With a full-time bookkeeper in your corner, you can feel at peace knowing this area of your enterprise is well taken care of as the business grows.

This does not give you permission to be disconnected from your business's finances. You can still be on top of it by asking for regular financial reports from the bookkeeper or your accountant. Or, if you're using reliable accounting software, you should have no problem generating financial reports regularly so you can have a bird's-eye view of how the business is doing financially.

Bookkeeping can still be a collaborative effort, even if you outsource or delegate it to somebody else. This is because that person doesn't know your business as well and as intimately as you do. So, sometimes, you will probably need to coordinate with your assigned bookkeeper and continue to stay abreast of your business's finances through regular updates.

Another advantage of hiring a bookkeeper is avoiding costly recording mistakes, especially with information pertaining to tax returns and payroll. Risks for such become higher the more complex, and numerous your business's financial transactions become. By hiring someone to focus on nothing else but bookkeeping, you enjoy the benefit of proper recording of financial transactions without stressing over it yourself.

But What About Accounting?

Regardless of the simplicity or complexity of your business's financial transactions, hiring an accountant is very important. The main reason for this is to ensure timely and proper filing of your business's taxes. While bookkeeping is a fairly simple task, which only becomes more and more complex as the business grows, tax accounting is something else. It requires specialized knowledge of tax regulations to ensure perfect compliance with tax authorities while minimizing tax liabilities.

Chapter 4: Small Business Tax Deductions

Every business owner wants to maximize profits. Who doesn't want to? There are many ways to do it, but one of the most common is by minimizing tax liabilities by claiming tax deductions. These are expenses that businesses can use to reduce their taxable income and, therefore, the taxes they must pay. A big chunk of tax accounting revolves around the ability to identify and claim allowable tax deductions. That is why it is important for you to understand this as a business owner.

Allowed Deductions

What makes certain business expenses tax deductible? The IRS has two important characteristics: these must be ordinary and necessary for the business. A business expense is considered common if it is one that other businesses in the same industry or niche also incur in normal operations. A business expense is considered necessary if it is appropriate and helpful to the business.

For proper tax accounting, you should be able to differentiate tax-deductible business expenses from:

- Cost of goods sold, particularly for trading businesses

- Personal expenses

- Capital expenses

Cost of Goods Sold (COGS)

Suppose you are engaged in a trading business, i.e., one that buys and sells goods or is a manufacturer. You will need to know your inventory value at the start and end of every taxable year to determine the cost of the goods sold. The only exception to this is if you are a small business taxpayer. We'll get into more detail about this later on.

For determining the cost of goods sold for your taxable year, you may include other types of expenses. The total cost of the goods your business sold will be deducted from its gross annual sales to determine the taxable year's gross profits, but if you include certain business expenses as part of CGS, you forfeit the right to use it as a deductible business expense later on for income tax filing purposes. Business expenses you can include as part of the cost of goods sold are:

- Purchase cost or cost of production, including freight and storage charges

- Direct labor costs for people who worked directly into acquiring or producing sold units, including annuity plan or pension contributions

- Overhead costs

Based on uniform capitalization guidelines, businesses need to capitalize on direct costs and indirect costs for specific resale or production activities. But if the business is a small, registered taxpayer, it is exempted. The most common indirect costs for goods sold include:

- Rentals

- Interest on borrowed money

- Taxes paid

- Warehousing costs

- Repackaging costs

- Processing

- Administrative expenses

Now, let us clarify who is a small business taxpayer is so you can determine if you qualify as one. Starting the tax year ending December 31, 2017, The IRS defines small business taxpayers as those that:

- Have an average annual gross revenue of $25 million or less for the last three tax years

- Are not considered as tax shelters, as defined under section 448(d)(3) of the Internal Revenue Code

So, let's say you qualify as a small business taxpayer. In that case, you have the option to adapt or change the accounting method used for accounting your business inventories like non-incidental materials and supplies or to conform to how you normally treat inventories in an applicable financial statement (Section 451(b)(3)). And if you don't have an applicable financial statement, your business can use an accounting method for inventories that conforms to your books and records prepared consistent with its accounting procedures (Section 471(c)(1)).

Capital Expenses

Capital expenses refer to those that are associated with acquiring or improving your business's fixed assets such as equipment, properties, and renovations. For expenses like these, the appropriate accounting or bookkeeping treatment should be to capitalize on them instead of treating them as deductible expenses. What does this mean?

Let's take a look at your business's utilities expenses, say electricity bills for the office. Since these are considered as common and necessary, you can claim them as tax deductions to reduce taxable income.

Now, let's say you bought a brand-new air-conditioning unit for $1,000 to replace the old and dilapidated one at the office. Because this is considered a fixed or long-term asset, you cannot consider its purchase cost as an expense you can claim as a tax deduction. Instead of recording a $1000 expense for the taxable year, you will record an increase in your business's furniture and equipment account. The matching accounting entry would either be a $1000 reduction in cash or a $1000 increase in current liabilities.

The only time you can use this as a tax-deductible expense is when you depreciate it across is estimated useful life. Let's say your accounting policy is to depreciate fixed assets using a straight-line method for five years. This means that for this air conditioning unit, the associated depreciation expense every taxable year is $200. This is the amount you can claim as a tax-deductible expense every taxable year for the next five years.

There are three general types of capitalized costs. These are improvements to the property or operating premises, business assets (such as the new air-conditioning unit), and business startup costs. Speaking of the latter, Chapters 7 and 8 of IRS Publication 535 on Business Expenses provides clear guidelines on what specific business startup costs you can claim outright or on an amortized basis as tax-deductible expenses.

Personal and Business Expenses

As a general guideline, you cannot claim personal, family, and living expenses as tax deductions, but there are certain exceptions. For example, if you incur expenses partially for business and partially for personal purposes, you can divide it into business and personal parts and use the former as tax deductions.

Allow me to illustrate more clearly. Let's say for the entire year; you spent $1000 on gasoline for your car. You use the car for personal and official business functions, and let's assume that out of the 10,000 total miles for the taxable year, 4,000 of them were used for business. This means 40% of the gasoline expenses can be attributed to your business's operations, and thus, you can claim a $400 tax deduction for your cars and gasoline expenses.

For more details on segregating personal and business expenses and allocations for tax deductions, check out Chapter 4 of the IRS' Publication 535 on Business Expenses.

Using Your Home for Business

You may deduct expenses related to your abode for business when you dedicate a specific area as an office, production area, etc. A few of the home-related costs you can include as tax deductions include:

- Interest on the mortgage
- Home insurance
- Utility bills
- Repair works
- Depreciation

For more information on the specifics of using your home for business and how to deduct related expenses from taxable income, check out the IRS' Publication 587 on the Business Use of Your Home and Home Office Deduction.

Using Your Car for Business

If you are using your car for business, you can deduct Its related expenses from taxable income, but if you use it both for personal and business purposes, you can only deduct a certain amount of the expenses based on actual mileage. How does this look like?

Let's say you spent a total of $1000 on your vehicle for gasoline and repairs this month. If the total mileage for the period is 1000 miles and 600 were for business-related trips, it means you can only use 60% of the $1000 - or $600 - as taxable income deductions.

If you want more information on how to compute for allowable tax deductions on your personal vehicle, check out the IRS' Publication 463 on Travel, Entertainment, Gift, and Car Expenses. To know the current and prior years' mileage rates based on the IRS regulations, you can check out its Standard Mileage Rates.

Other Kinds of Business Expenses

- Employee salaries

- Insurance premiums for the business

- Interest on money borrowed from banks and other financial institutions

- Rent payments

- Retirement accounts

- Taxes

Common Tax Deductions for Small Businesses

As a small business, you can claim several expenses as legitimate deductions to your taxable income, so you will pay the lowest possible income taxes. What are these expenses? Here's a list of a few of the most common ones.

Business-Related Food Expenses

For qualified food and drink purchases related to your small business's conduct, you can deduct as much as 50% of the total amount. What makes such purchases qualified?

The first requirement is that obviously, it was related to the business. Family meals and treating friends out to lunch do not count. But if it is used to meet with and treat a potential client to coffee or dinner, it is considered business-related.

The second requirement is that such purchases need to be properly supported by documents like official receipts or invoices. These pieces of information must be on the supporting papers:

- Location off the meal

- date when the meal took place

- How are you or your business's representative related to the people or person the meal was shared with

- The meal's total cost

The most practical and accurate way to be on top of your business's meal expenses is by keeping official receipts and writing notes at the back.

Business Travel Expenses

You can deduct 100% of all qualified business-related travel expenses when you file your business's income tax returns. These include plane tickets, hotel check-ins, meals, and car rental expenses, among others.

How to make sure these are really qualified? The most important characteristics include:

- The trip is absolutely needed for your business

- You must travel outside of your tax-registered business address, i.e., outside the city or state where your small business conducts its normal operations

- The trip must last longer than one normal business day

- The travel requires sleeping or resting on the route

Business Related Vehicle Use

If the vehicle is used solely for the business, you may deduct 100% of all related expenses. But if it is used for both business and personal activities, you may only claim the business-related portion of the expenses.

You can do this in two ways: using actual mileage for the period or using The IRS prescribed standard mileage rates per mile driven. As the name of the first option implies, you will compute the percentage of business-related mileage to the total distance for the period and multiply it by the period's vehicle use related total expenses. If you choose to use the IRS' standard mileage rates, just multiply it by the period's total mileage.

Insurance Premiums

Whatever you pay to ensure your business's assets, you can use as a legitimate tax deduction come filing time. But if you are holding office at home or use part of it to run your business, you can use your renter's insurance costs as taxable income deductions.

Expenses Related to Running a Home Office

Based on the simplified home office expense guidelines issued by the IRS, you can deduct $5 per square foot of the area of your home dedicated to running a small business or doing freelancing work up to a maximum area of 300 square feet. To qualify for this deduction, two conditions must be satisfied.

First, the area must be for the exclusive use of the business only. Here, you cannot clean deductions if you run your small business from your dining room because it is not exclusively used for the business. The dining room will still be there even if you didn't run your business from home.

Second, the whole office area must be used regularly as the primary place of your business's operations. It must be your headquarters.

Supplies

For as long as you use office supplies for your small business in the year in which you bought them, you can claim their purchase costs as tax deductions. These include:

- Paper

- Pens

- Printer cartridges

- Paper clips

- Other work-related consumable items

Always remember to keep the official receipts to make sure proper documentation and support for filing them as tax deductions.

Communications Expenses

If your small business is heavily reliant on using the phone and the Internet, then you can claim expenses related to these as tax deductions, but if you use them for both personal and business activities, you can only claim a certain percentage of the expenses attributable to your small business as tax deductions.

Let's say your monthly Internet bills average around $50. If you use it for business three-fourths of the time, then you can claim 75% of that monthly expense - or 37.5 dollars - as tax deductions.

Bank Fees and Interest on Loans

If you fund part of your operations using bank financing, you can use the interest paid on borrowed money as tax deductions. If you have business-related credit cards, interest and charges on these qualify as tax deductions too. Again, the qualifier here is that they are directly related to your small business's operations.

Depreciation Expenses

These pertain to the annual writing off of the cost of big-ticket capital items like vehicles, equipment, and improvements done on the office's premises. Instead of deducting the entire cost as a onetime expense, assets like these are capitalized in your business's books of accounts. The entire cost is amortized over the next several years as depreciation expense.

The amount of depreciation expense claimed annually depends on the chosen method. The most common one is the straight-line method, which divides the total asset cost over its estimated useful life as expressed in several years.

For example, you spent $10,000 on improving a condominium unit used as your small business's primary office. Your estimated useful life for the improvements is ten straight-line depreciation expense using the straight-line method is $1000. This is the amount of depreciation on the asset you can claim as deductions when you file your business's annual income tax.

Service or Professional Fees

When your small business needs to hire professionals to help in its operations, you can use the money you pay them as tax deductions. These include the retainer fees of your accountant, lawyer, or bookkeeper, among others. You may also include tax-deductible service or professional fees or the cost of subscribing to an accounting or bookkeeping software such as QuickBooks.

If you need more information regarding tax-deductible professional or service fees, check out the IRS' guidelines for legal and professional fees.

Employee Salaries and Benefits

If your small business has employees, you may also claim their salaries, paid leaves, and other benefits as tax deductions if you meet several requirements. These include:

> • The employee is not an owner, partner, or member of the business

> • The salary paid is both necessary and reasonable

> • The employee was able to do his or her duties and responsibilities to the business

Donations to Charitable Institutions

If you have a philanthropic heart, your business may also benefit from helping qualified organizations. Your business may use qualified donations as tax deductions depending on its structure. If yours is a single proprietorship, partnership, or a limited liability corporation (LLC), you may claim the deductions on your personal tax returns. But if it's a corporation, you may claim the charitable donations on your business's corporate tax filings.

Learning Costs

You may use educational expenses meant for the business's economic benefit as legitimate deductions for your small business. What do these educational expenses look like?

If you are running a printing business and you enroll in a seminar that helps you learn how to use a cutting-edge graphic design software like Photoshop, you can use the fee as a tax deduction for your small business.

If you're operating a small coffee shop and you enroll in an Udemy course on how to brew the perfect coffee, you can claim the cost of the e-course when you file your or your business's tax returns.

These must help you become better at what you do for your business or maintain your expertise or qualifications. That way, the enterprise can grow. The following are education-related expenses that qualify as tax deductions for your small business:

- Courses and classes directly relevant to your business or line of work
- Webinars and seminars
- Subscriptions to publications related to your business or profession
- Books or e-books related to your industry

Dependent and Child Care

While these may look like personal expenses on the surface, you may claim them as tax-deductible expenses for your small business. For example, care-related costs for your children 12 years old or younger are eligible as tax-deductible expenses. If adult dependents require professional care because of mental or physical disabilities, such as your spouse or parents, you may also claim their professional care expenses. Ask for the deductions when you file your personal or business income tax returns.

Energy Efficiency-Related Costs

Believe it or not, The IRS gives credit to taxpayers who do their best to improve their home or office is energy efficiency. Expenses incurred for making the home or business premises more energy efficient entitle you or your small business a 30% tax credit or deduction. This means if you spent $1000 to install energy efficiency devices such as solar panels, wind turbines, or solar water heaters, you could claim a $300 tax deduction on this expense. For more details on this, the IRS provides details on home energy tax credits on their website.

Costs of Investments

Let us say you or your small business wants to take advantage of depressed stock prices to make extra income, and you borrow money to do so. You can claim the interest paid on loan as tax deductions, but you can only do so up to the amount of interest that does not exceed the investment's income. If interest amounted to $100, but the income is only $50, you can only claim $50 in interest expenses as tax deductions for the borrowed money.

Medical Expenses

Whether it's medical care expenses (including your doctor's professional fees, medicines, or home care costs) or insurance premiums, You can claim these expenses as deductions in your or your small business's tax returns. If you're self-employed and pay for your own Medicare, you can also claim dental and health care insurance premiums as deductions.

Property Taxes

When your small business pays real estate taxes at the local and state levels, you can claim them as valid tax deductions, but there is a maximum limit of $10,000 only.

Interest on Loans and Mortgages

If you borrowed money to finance the construction or improvement of your small business's office or your home, if you use it for running your enterprise, then you can claim interest payments as tax deductions. Even when you take out loans against your home or property equity, the interest on such a borrowed money can also be valid tax deductions.

Moving Expenses

If your business incurred moving expenses, then you may be able to use them as tax deductions, but it must first pass a distance test. The distance of your new business location from the old one must be at least 50 miles. Or if you move to a new home as part of your business operations, your new home must be at least the same distance away from your old one.

Retirement Account Contributions

If you are currently contributing to an IRA or an individual retirement account, you may use the number of your contributions as part of your tax deductions, especially if your small business is a sole proprietorship, partnership, or an LLC. This is because income earned from these types of businesses is taxed personally, i.e., you file their income taxes on your personal returns.

Marketing and Advertising Expenses

All expenses related to promoting and marketing your small business's products or services are tax deductible. These include website design, print and digital advertising, website maintenance, and business card printing.

Entertainment Expenses for Clients and Employees

As long as you discuss business with your clients during meetings, you may claim entertainment expenses of up to 50% of the actual amount. If you hold social events for your employees, you may even claim as much as 100% of the expenses as deductions.

Costs Related to Starting a Business

If you set up a new business on your latest tax year, you may claim up to $5000 in startup expenses related to it. These expenses include costs of training, travel, marketing, and other things necessary for setting up the new enterprise.

Chapter 5: Payroll Taxes Explained

If your small business employs people, then you must withhold, report, and remit the taxes on your employees' salaries to the IRS. Employment taxes aren't just limited to employees' income taxes but also cover their FICA taxes, e.g., Social Security and Medicare. When it comes to the latter, you, as an employer, don't just withhold and remit your employees' contributions but also pay your share. This is one of the most important aspects of your business because failure to comply with employment tax regulations can subject you and your business to substantial penalties.

Aside from your employees' salaries and FICA taxes, employment taxes also include FUTA (federal unemployment taxes paid solely by you as an employer) and state unemployment taxes paid both by you and your employees, depending on what state you're operating in.

With these types of taxes, you need to be familiar with certain mandatory activities. These include:

- Computation of all withholding taxes and other employment taxes

- Depositing of employment taxes according to set schedules unless you are a very small employer or business

- Reporting of employment taxes every quarter to the IRS. This covers all withholding income taxes and FICA taxes

- Annual reporting of employees' tax payments to both the employees and the Social Security Administration

- Annual FUTA reporting

- Reporting employment taxes at the state level

Mandatory Payroll Taxes

These taxes are mandatory upon you as an employer, and if you're not able to comply, tax authorities may penalize you. Payroll taxes can be classified as employee-paid, employer-paid, or both. But regardless, it's your responsibility as an employer to make sure these are deposited with the proper tax authorities.

Federal Income Taxes

These refer to income taxes levied at the national level, which means income earners need to file and pay them to the IRS regardless of the state they're in. This includes Social Security and Medicare taxes (FICA), and for some employees, this also covers additional taxes for Medicare.

State Income Taxes

Most states mandate employers to withhold state income taxes from their employees' paychecks except for:

- Alaska
- Florida
- Nevada
- South Dakota
- Texas
- Washington

- Wyoming

Also, New Hampshire and Tennessee don't tax wages through 2020.

City Income Taxes

In a few cities, income earners pay income taxes three times: at the Federal, state, and city levels! For example, Philadelphia and New York levy their own set of income taxes on their resident income earners. If you're an employer in cities like these, you have even more income taxes to withhold from your employees' salaries.

Other Payroll Taxes

For certain locations, employers need to withhold additional taxes from employees' monetary benefits. These include short-term disability, paid family leaves, and unemployment benefits.

FICA (Federal Insurance Contributions Act) Taxes

These refer to Medicare and Social Security taxes. These are paid by both employers and employees, with each party contributing 6.2% of the employee's salary to his or her Social Security account up to a maximum annual wage limit of $137,700 in 2020 and an extra 1.45% to cover Medicare.

FUTA (Federal Unemployment Tax Act)

While the Federal government is not responsible for giving benefits to the unemployed, it helps state governments provide them to their constituents who were laid off from work. It does so via the Federal Unemployment Tax Act, which requires employers to contribute 6% of an employee's salary, but employers may get state unemployment tax credits of up to 5.4%, which can help significantly reduce their burden to only 0.6% of their employees' salaries or up to a maximum FUTA payment of only $42.

Your credit may shrink - and your contributions as an employer may rise - when the state you're operating in borrows from the Federal government for unemployment benefits but has not paid back the loan. Your state will be classified as a credit reduction state, which means your FUTA payments as an employer will increase.

State Unemployment Taxes

Your state gives unemployment benefits to qualified employees who were terminated involuntarily, i.e., not for a cause such as gross misconduct or furloughs. To do this, it may impose unemployment taxes on employers like you.

State unemployment taxes are similar to insurance policies because rates are based on the number of former employees' claims. The more claims your employees made in the past, the higher your state unemployment taxes will be. Your state will tell you the tax rate for your business.

Extra Medicare Taxes

When your employee's salary exceeds the $200,000 threshold, you must withhold extra contributions from his or her pay to cover extra or additional Medicare taxes. The additional tax equals 0.9% of income above $200,000 for those who aren't married, more than $250,000 for those who file jointly with their spouses, and over $125,000 for married taxpayers filing separately from their spouses.

Fortunately for you, employers have to withhold only it from the employee's salary. So, your business need not shell out money for additional Medicare taxes.

Your Payroll Responsibilities as an Employer

As an employer, you're responsible for filing employment tax returns and remitting withheld taxes to the government according to specific deadlines. If you don't, you risk being subjected to failure to file and pay penalties, which can be substantial.

Also, it's important to remember that you or other people in your business who are responsible for failure to file and pay employment taxes may be subjected to a 100% personal liability. When you or that responsible person willfully refuses to deposit the taxes, it will trigger what is called *the trust fund recovery penalty*. Because these penalties may involve substantial amounts, plus serious tarnish on your business's reputation, you will need to take these responsibilities seriously.

As an employer, your extensive payroll tax responsibilities include:

- Computing how much federal, state, and local income taxes to withhold from your employees

- Depositing income taxes withheld to the proper tax authorities

- Filing various tax returns for payroll reporting purposes

Computing Employer Payroll Taxes

You can use the IRS' Form W-4 to determine the payroll taxes your business needs to withhold and deposit every month. It gives you information about the employee's marital status and if you must withhold additional taxes for him or her. If the form isn't available, the default or assumed marital status of the employee is "single," and there's no need to withhold additional taxes.

If you or your business uses an external payroll management service like Paychex, you can delegate payroll tax calculations to it. But if you're doing payroll in-house, you can use accounting software or the IRS' Circular E, which provides useful tables, to determine the payroll taxes.

Required Payroll Tax Forms

You need not use specialized forms to determine the amount of payroll taxes for the period. The same goes for when depositing them to the tax authorities. You will need to use specific forms for filing them, however.

For filing federal level employment taxes, you or your business will need to use these forms:

- Form 940 or your annual FUTA tax return as an employer.

- Form 941 or your quarterly tax return to report your share of the FICA taxes withheld from employees and your employer contribution. For 2020, and possibly for 2021, you can use this form to avail of credits for employment taxes to cover payment for specific employee benefits due to COVID-19, such as mandatory sick leaves and family leaves.

- Form 7200 for advanced crediting of employment taxes, should employment taxes be insufficient to cover the above-mentioned payments to employees due to the pandemic.

- Form 943, which is the annual return you will file for agricultural employees.

- Form 944, which you can use to pay annual employment taxes instead of paying them according to schedule if your small business is eligible.

- form 945, which is a federal income tax return for reporting events unrelated to payroll like pension distributions.

As an employer, you will also be required to report Social Security deductions from your employees' salaries. You will file these with the Social Security Administration using these forms:

- Form W-2, which you'll give to your employees

- Form W-3 with the Social Security Administration, which is a transmittal form for summarizing all the attached copies of W-2 forms for the period

Depositing Employer Taxes

To avoid being penalized, you must make sure these are paid to or deposited with the appropriate tax authorities on time, every time. The taxes to be remitted will determine your deadlines. If you are a small business, you must make monthly deposits at the minimum. For very large employers, they need to make deposits every two weeks.

For your payments, you may use either form 941 or 944. The application form will depend on specific conditions, details of which are available on pages 25 to 26 of the IRS' Publication 15 on depositing taxes.

During the COVID-19 pandemic, you have the option to defer the depositing and paying your employer's share of Social Security. This covers the period starting from 27 March 2020 until 31 December 2020. If you avail of this option, you may deposit at least 50% of the deferred amount by 31 December 2021 and the remaining balance by 31 December 2022. If you're able to meet these payment deadlines, they will be considered as timely payments, and you will not be subject to late payment penalties.

For all payroll taxes, you must deposit them electronically using the Federal Electronic Tax Payment System or EFTPS. As a small employer, you may also use the EFTPS to pay their employment taxes simultaneously with filing their annual employment tax returns.

Employer Tax Return Filings

Just like tax payments, you also need to file the returns based on certain schedules set by the IRS. Failure to do so can get your business in trouble. Fortunately, small business owners like you have the option of doing it manually by going to the tax authorities' offices or agents or by doing it electronically from the comfort and convenience of your office or home.

How often should you file employment taxes? For most employers, annual filings are the norm. But with the federal returns, using Form 941, quarterly filings are required.

State-level returns are filed differently. Check with your state's tax authorities or finance department.

Form W-4 is also called the employee's withholding certificate; it's one that your employees need to fill up to give you information you will need to compute for their withholding taxes properly. And for new employees, you must make them fill up Form I-9 so you can determine if they legally may work in the United States.

You may also want to consider asking your employees to fill out Form 8850. If a new employee belongs to be federally specified demographic or ethnic group and if you want to take advantage of it by availing of the government's Work Opportunity Tax Credit, this is the form you will need to submit.

What About Compensation of Independent Contractors or Self-Employed Individuals

The first thing you will need to consider is that self-employed individuals and independent contractors are *not* employees. As such, you're not responsible for withholding employment taxes on any payments you make to them, but it is still best for you as an employer to make sure that the individual you're dealing with is properly classified as such.

These individuals pay and file their own self-employment taxes on their net earnings through self-employment. Basically, they pay both the employee and employer's share of the FICA. If this self-employed person also earns wages from another job, these are coordinated with their self-employment taxes so the right ceiling can be applied to the wage base.

If annual payments made to such individuals exceed $600, you will need to file an annual information return using the IRS' Form 1099-NEC. This will report your payments to both the tax authorities and individual contractors you paid.

Chapter 6: Why a Business Entity is Important

As a businessperson, the type of business or industry to get into isn't the only thing you have to decide on. You will also need to think carefully about the structure or entity your business will be. Why?

There are two very important reasons: taxes and personal liability. Believe it or not, the business entity you register can directly affect the kinds and amount of taxes you will need to pay. For example, structuring your business as a company or a corporation entitles it to a flat income tax rate. And if you structure your business as a sole proprietorship or a partnership, taxes on income from these will be filed under your own, and thus, you will be paying graduated income tax rates.

Depending on your expected or target annual net income, one type of tax rate can be beneficial compared to the other. For businesses, paying a flat corporate tax rate can be more tax-efficient compared to paying an individual but graduated one. This is especially so when the business is making lots of money, just like the top American companies do.

But if your income isn't as high as major corporations' annual profits, paying taxes on income based on an increasing rate may be more practical. If you're earning $10,000,000 in net income annually, you will be paying the top rate for individual income taxes. However, you may have to pay more than half of your income in taxes because of the tax bracket. But if you are a flat corporate tax rate, you won't be paying as many taxes because regardless of the size of your income, the rate is fixed.

Also, your personal liability for claims made against your business is contingent on the business structure you adopt. Case in point, sole proprietorships. If you structure your business like this and it goes bankrupt, its creditors and other parties with a financial claim on it can go after your personal assets. But if you establish a corporation instead, such parties can only go after the business's assets to settle their claims.

Common Types of Business Entities

While we will be going into more detail about the business entities you can establish in the United States, here are the most common business entities in the United States:

- Sole proprietorships
- Partnerships
- Limited Liability Corporations (LLCs)
- Corporations (C And S)

Business Entities: The Accounting Concept

The business entity concept of accounting also called an economic entity or the separate entity concept, requires that all financial transactions of a business be distinguished and separated from that of its owners or other businesses. It means that each business's finances must not be commingled with anyone or anything else's.

What does this mean? When funds go in and out of your business, their movements must be recorded in their own books of accounts or accounting records. As a business owner, you can – and you should - apply this concept to your business regardless of its structure or entity type. Doing this can make the accounting and bookkeeping process is so much easier and accurate.

Other ways to practice the business entity accounting concept include using a dedicated credit card and opening a bank account under the business name.

Now, why is this concept so important? Why do business organizations go for this accounting setup? Here are four very good reasons.

Clear and Accurate Information

When you keep separate accounting and financial records for your business, it will be easy for you to get clear and accurate information on its financial health and performance. If you're operating multiple businesses, doing so allows you to compare each business's financial health and performance easily. You can also more easily get an idea if your business is performing at par with the industry or its peers. These information can help you manage your business well and lower its risks.

Easy and Simple Keeping of Records and Auditing

When your business is financial, and accounting records are segregated from your personal ones and your other business's, you will have no problems keeping track of its records. And during audit seasons, your auditor can quickly and accurately complete the process.

Contrast this when your business's financial and accounting records co-mingle with your own and/or those for other businesses you own. When you want to consider revenues for the month, you must make the extra effort to segregate the business income from your personal income, especially if you earn income from other sources. To check the profitability of your enterprise and the financial and accounting records of your other businesses are commingled, you cannot determine whether it's making money or not without having to go through the painstaking process of segregating one from the other.

Easy and Accurate Filing of Income Taxes

For the same reason as above, ensuring that each business entity's financial and accounting records are segregated from your personal ones or those of your other business's guarantees you or your tax accountant will not have a hard time computing, depositing, and filing the right income tax returns.

Hassle-Free Liquidation

Without meaning to sound pessimistic, there is always the possibility for a business to go belly under, close shop, and be liquidated. Keeping financial and accounting records separate makes it much easier to determine how the owners will be compensated if there are remaining funds after liquidation.

Choosing the Appropriate Business Entity

While there are no hard and fast rules for choosing "the one," there are things that you can do to maximize your chances of choosing the most beneficial business entity for the one you plan to start.

Know the Tax Consequences

Remember that one of the two reasons you should carefully choose a business entity is taxes. True, some business entities are more tax-efficient compared to others under certain situations. While you should always consult a tax expert such as a business lawyer or tax accountant for making this very important decision, here are some basic information about the relationship between business entities and taxation you need to know.

• If you choose to set up a sole proprietorship or a general partnership business, it will be considered a "disregarded entity" for taxation purposes. This means that you, as an owner, will file its income and expenses under your personal tax returns. You will pay its income taxes.

• If you set up a business using a corporation, the way it will be taxed will depend on the corporation you choose. A-C corporation is taxed differently from an S corporation, details of which you will learn later in succeeding chapters.

• If you set up a limited liability company or corporation (LLC), it will be taxed in the same way as sole proprietorships or partnerships are. However, it may also be taxed as a corporation, and we will discuss these nuances in the chapters on corporations.

Understand the Impact on Personal Liability

Are you comfortable knowing that your business is creditors and third parties with claims against it can go after your personal assets If it fails to settle its obligations? Or are you the type of person who wants to keep your personal riches safe from such claims? By understanding the impact on your personal liability, you can choose the kind of business entity in line with your preference on this matter.

Speaking of personal liability, you must also know such protections aren't absolute. Yes, certain types of business entities can give you protection from certain lawsuits or judgments against your business, but there are limits, too.

For example, a corporate structure can protect your personal bank account and other assets if your business cannot pay its debts. But it cannot protect you from lawsuits and claims arising from negligence or malicious actions done through the business.

Also, no business structure can protect you from losing your investment due to disasters or accidents such as wildfires or cyclones. If your business suffers a lot or has to close due to severe damage from such events, you will bear those losses as the owner. That is why regardless of the structure or entity you choose; you must get insurance for your business.

Consider Other Out-of-State Incorporation Costs

As you do your research to guide you in choosing your business's appropriate entity, you will probably come across information on incorporating in other states such as Delaware, Nevada, or Wyoming. This is because states like these provide huge income tax savings, ultimately maximizing the returns on investments.

However, incorporating in such states, especially if you're not from there, may turn out to be more complicated and expensive compared to incorporating in your home state. This can be especially true if yours is a small business. For one, out of state incorporations will require you to maintain registered agents in your home state and the state you plan to incorporate in. And aside from these additional costs, your paperwork may also double. This is because you'll have two submit annual reports and be annual fees in both states.

Contrast that with incorporating your business in your home state. Unless you expect to make huge profits as big corporations do, the amount you'll probably save in taxes may not be enough to make it worthwhile to incorporate outside, considering out-of-state incorporation costs such as the ones mentioned above. While the taxes may be higher, your paperwork will be a lot less complicated, and you will not have to spend double for things like registered agents.

Prepare Formal Agreements With Your Business Partners

Gone were the days when most business owners easily get along with each other, work problems out, and can trust each other's words. That is why for your protection and theirs, you should prepare and sign formal agreements that cover the most important aspects of your business. From key responsibilities to expected deliverables, details must be printed and signed so that if disagreements happen, there will be an objective basis to settle them.

That is why regardless of the business structure you or you and your partners choose, you must have a formal agreement in place already. Some important things to cover include:

- Resolution of potential conflicts

- What to do when one owner or partners die

- When and how to accept new owners

- How to divide profits and losses among owners or partners

The type of formal agreement will depend on the kind of business entity or structure you choose. It can be a partnership agreement, an operating agreement, or a buy and sell agreement. And while coming up with a solid and documented agreement may require significant time and effort, it will more than make up for those things when conflicts or disagreements arise, and they help resolve them quickly and amicably.

Chapter 7: Limited Liability Company

A limited liability company or LLC is a kind of business entity based in the United States wherein the owners have no personal liability for money that the company owes to creditors and other claimants. These are considered hybrid companies that bring the characteristics of a partnership or sole proprietorship and corporation together. How?

Its limited liability characteristic is taken from a Corporation. But filing of its income taxes through its owners' personal returns is something taken from sole proprietorships or partnerships.

Generally, , limited liability companies are businesses permitted under State statutes. LLCs are governed differently from state to state. That is why when setting up an LLC in your specific state; you must do diligent research specific to where you are.

As an owner of an LLC, you are neither called a proprietor, partner, nor stockholder. Instead, you will be called a *member.*

Different states have different regulations for limited liability corporations. Many don't impose restrictions on ownership. This means anybody can be an LLC member, including corporations, individuals, and foreigners, or foreign entities. A limited liability

Corporation can become a member of another LLC. The only restrictions as to membership of this type of business entity pertain to banks and insurance companies. They cannot be members of, or form limited liability corporations.

Compared to a partnership, an LLC is a more formal type of business entity. Instead of a mere partnership agreement, LLC members need to create articles of organization and file them with the state in which the business will be located. Compared to a corporation, setting up a limited liability corporation is much easier with more protection and flexibility.

As an LLC, your business may elect not to pay federal income taxes. Instead, it may report its profits or losses under your and other members' personal tax returns. It may also be classified differently, like a corporation. But as far as creditor protection for members is concerned, it is only available if the company meets legal and reportorial requirements and if no fraud is committed. Otherwise, parties with valid financial claims against the company can go after its members' personal assets.

If you get wages from your LLC, it will be part of its operating expenses and, thus, may be considered or claimed as a valid tax-deductible expense for the business.

Setting up a Limited Liability Corporation

The requirements for doing so vary across different states. Still, many have similar requirements, such as choosing a name for the enterprise at the start of the setting up process.

After you have chosen your LLC's formal name, you must formally document its articles of organization and, then file them with the state in which you're registering it. The articles must contain important information about you and/or other members, such as:

- Names
- Addresses

- Rights

- Powers

- Duties

- Liabilities

- Duties and responsibilities

Other important pieces of information required under the articles of organization are the name of your chosen registered agent and the business's statement of purpose. When filing this document, it must come with a fee you must directly pay to the state. Additional fees and paperwork are also required when submitting at the federal level to get an employer identification number (EIN).

LLCs: A Short History

Wyoming, every first state that authorized the creation of limited liability companies. It did so in 1977.

Between 1960 to 1997, unincorporated business associations were classified for federal tax purposes by what is now known as the "Kintner regulations." The Internal Revenue Service promulgated these regulations in 1960, and these set a complicated system of six-factor tests to determine whether these businesses will be taxed as partnerships or as corporations.

The Wyoming limited liability corporation statute was crafted by the Wyoming legislature to take advantage of an important shortcoming in the Kintner regulations: all six-factors must be treated with equal importance. Thus, this feature of the Kintner regulations made it possible to create a business entity with both limited liability and pass-through tax treatment.

Outside Wyoming, other states weren't as excited to adopt LLCs as a type of business entity. It was because, for several years, there were still doubts whether an LLC in Wyoming would be taxed like a partnership under the Kintner regulations. It was only after the IRS decided with finality in 1998, via its Revenue Ruling 88-76, that LLCs are taxable as partnerships did other states warmed up to LLCs in their own jurisdictions and promulgated their own LLC laws. By 1996, all 50 states have promulgated their own LLC-related laws.

In 1995, however, the IRS concluded that the prevalent enactment of LLC laws all over the United States actually undercut the Kintner regulations. Thus, it enforced new rules and regulations using a CTB (check the box) classification system for entity elections that became effective across the country on 1 January 1997.

Is an LLC the Right Business Structure for You?

To determine whether this is the appropriate business entity for you, carefully evaluating the benefits and detriments of an LLC. Let's start with the benefits.

LLC Benefits

The primary benefit of an LLC can give you is liability protection. Because these are considered a corporation, they offer its owners or members the same benefits as the corporate veil: their financial obligations are separate from its members or owners. That is why when your LLC goes bankrupt, its creditors cannot go after your assets.

However, liability protection isn't absolute. If liability to another party arises because of willful neglect or malicious intent, then the aggrieved parties or claimants may go after you. Fortunately, getting into this trouble with an LLC, pretty hard to do. Unless you have malicious intentions from the get-go or are negligent as an entrepreneur, the liability protection offered by an LLC should be enough.

Another advantage associated with an LLC business is pass-through taxation. This means the business itself does not have to pay income taxes, but instead, those will be passed through for your personal income tax returns. How is this an advantage?

If you plan to claim your share of all the business's net income regularly, by withdrawing it from the business, you will only be taxed once. Remember that as a limited liability Corporation with a pass-through taxation benefit, the business is income is taxed on a personal level or through your own income tax returns. But if you plan to do this through a corporation set up, you may be subject to double taxation. Why?

With a regular corporation, the business files and pays its own tax returns separate from its owners. When the net income after tax is distributed to the stockholders in the form of dividends, the Internal Revenue Service considers it as personal income for the owners. Stockholders will need to file their dividend income in their personal income tax returns.

Let's say corporation A registered the taxable net income of $10,000,000. If the corporate tax rate is 30%, it must pay a $3,000,000 income tax, resulting in a net income after tax of $7,000,000.

If the company distributes its income completely as dividends to its shareholders, the latter must report and file income taxes on those dividends. So, in effect, the same income was taxed twice: First on the corporate level and second on the personal level.

But if the company was an LLC, its income will be passed through but its owners. It will only be taxed on a personal level and not on a corporate level, too. Using the same figures, income taxes on the $10,000,000 pretax income will be filed and paid under your and other members' – if any – personal returns. In effect, taxation only happens once.

Simplicity is another key benefit of choosing an LLC business entity. Compared to other types of similar businesses, it requires much less paper and administrative works.

With an LLC, you may also enjoy a good amount of flexibility. For example, you may elect to be a single-member or multiple-member entity. And speaking of flexibility, choosing this structure gives you tax payment options. You can be taxed in several ways, e.g., as an S or C corporation, each with its distinct advantages depending on your preferences and goals.

For example, electing to be taxed as an S corporation gives you the peculiar advantage of separating the income you earn through the business into salary and distributions or your share of its profits. For FICA (Federal Insurance Contributions Act) taxes such as social security and Medicare, only your salary is subject to them. Your distributions are exempted.

Why's this important? The main benefit of this is you can minimize FICA taxes and, therefore, maximize your take-home income.

However, you must exercise great caution when using this strategy. It's because the IRS mandates paying yourself a reasonable salary for playing an active role in your LLC. If you try to minimize your salary just to minimize self-employment taxes while maximizing distributions, they'll discover and will penalize you. Paying yourself a $5,000 annual salary with a $70,000 distribution attempts to circumvent the rules, and you'll pay a heftier price than the right FICA taxes.

Another advantage is that it also lends more credibility to your small business. Compared to a single proprietorship or partnership, an LLC is considered a more "formal" business entity. While this benefit is more psychological than practical, it's still a benefit, nevertheless. If your prospects and clients think more highly of your business because of this impression, it's definitely a good thing.

Finally, forming an LLC may give your business greater access to financing, e.g., business loans, because doing so enables it to record a credit history. For securing financing, institutions are very particular with credit history.

Potential LLC Disadvantages

Yes, LLCS can give multiple benefits for you as a business owner. However, it's not perfect, and it also has its share of disadvantages. One of them is passed through taxation.

Wait, didn't we just learn that pass-through taxation can be one of its greatest benefits? It is if you plan to claim or withdraw the business's net income regularly. But what if you decide to just leave it in the business to finance future expansions? If you plan to do this and choose an LLC, you will pay income taxes on its income whether or not you keep the income inside the business or take it out for personal uses. Many business owners with long-term plans of growing their enterprises do not choose LLCs.

Another potential disadvantage to this business structure is dependence on the LLC for filing of personal income taxes. This is because all members need to wait until the business gives them K-1 forms necessary for filing their personal income tax returns. However, this may not be that big of a deal if you are a single-member LLC.

To LLC or Not to LLC

To help you decide whether this is the appropriate business entity for you, the following are indicators it may be so:

> • You feel more secure knowing your personal assets and liabilities are separate from your business'

> • You don't like lots of paperwork and formalities

> • Your business is likely to incur losses in the first two years, and you want to use them as deferred tax assets for your personal returns

> • You want to minimize self-employment taxes as a solopreneur or working owner

How an LLC is Taxed

But the real issue here is tax accounting, and as such, what are the tax implications of operating an LLC? This business is a pass-through entity, resembling more of a single proprietorship than a corporation. Basically, members or owners pay income taxes on their share of the entity's profits, i.e., income tax returns are passed to the owners/members instead of the business filing and paying its own.

Just like sole proprietorships, you will include your share of the LLC's profits in your personal tax returns regardless if you pull it out or leave it in the business's account. For example, your LLC earns a taxable profit of $60,000 in 2019, and regardless of your business retains it, or you pull it out, you'll pay taxes on the entire $60,000 for that year.

You will also have to pay self-employment taxes if you are actively participating in your LLC. This includes social security and Medicare.

If you elect for a single-member LLC, you will be taxed as a sole proprietorship by the IRS. Its income will be filed under your personal tax returns.

Being the only member or owner of the LLC, you will report all income or losses of the business using Schedule C together with your 1040 tax return. And whether or not you retained the earnings for future company expansion or withdrew them for your personal use, you will need to file and pay income taxes on these.

If you elect for a multi-owner or member LLC with other business partners, it'll be taxed as a partnership. The only difference with a single-member LLC is that instead of only you are filing the business's income taxes in your personal returns, all of you will be doing so according to your share of the income, i.e., your respective distributive shares. These are set out in the operating agreement of your LLC.

For most LLCs, their operating agreements designate each member's distributive share in the company's net income under his or her percentage ownership or capital contribution. Let's say that your LLC has four members: you, Christine, Jacob, and Jenny. Of the business's $50,000 capital contributions, yours is $12,500, Christine's is $10,000, Jacob's is $15,000, and Jenny's is $12,500. The distributive share of each member in the company's net income is 25% for you, 20% for Christine, 30% for Jacob, and 25% for Jenny.

However, members of a multi-member LLC may agree on a distributive share scheme of their choosing. It may not necessarily be according to capital contribution but based on other considerations also like responsibilities in the business's operations and the number of sales they bring into the business every year. Any allocation scheme not based on actual capital contribution is called "special allocations" these have to be in line with the IRS' rules.

But regardless of the chosen allocation scheme, each member must file and pay taxes on their proportionate share of the LLC's net income even if they choose not to withdraw their share of it from the business.

And while a multi-member LLC isn't required to pay income taxes, it still needs to file IRS form 1065, just the same one that partnerships use. Why? This informational return must guarantee that each individual LLC member is reporting and filing the right income taxes. You may think of it as a check and balance of sorts for tax authorities.

The company must give its members a Schedule K-1, which breaks down every LLC member's distributive share of profits and losses. The members need to attach this form with their individual form 1040, with their attached Schedule E.

Self-Employment Taxes

As an LLC member, you are considered a self-employed businessperson and not as an employee of the company. It will not withhold Social Security and Medicare taxes for you, but instead, you will have to estimate, pay, and file them personally. The equivalent of employment taxes for people like you are self-employment taxes.

The IRS requires that any business owner that works for or helps manage an enterprise must pay self-employment taxes based on their distributive share of the LLC's net income. But if you are not involved in managing or operating the business and have chosen to just invest the money instead, you may be exempted from paying these taxes. The rules and regulations and governing self-employment taxes are complex, but it's safe to say that if you are actively participating in the LLC's operations, you must pay self-employment taxes on your share of the net income.

You other LLC members must report self-employment taxes using Schedule SE, which you will submit annually with your 1040 tax return. Compared to employees, your self-employment taxes are practically double the amount. This is because, as a self-employed businessperson, you are both the employee and the employer. You're responsible for the contributions of both.

Deductions and Expenses

You may significantly reduce the amount of taxable income you must report to the IRS by the ducting or writing off legitimate expenses related to conducting business from your business income. Some of these include the costs of starting up the business, vehicle expenses, advertising and promotion, and travel expenses, among others. To make sure you're able to maximize tax deductions, it's always best to consult with a tax accountant.

Taxes and Fees at the State Level

Usually, individual states impose taxes on LLCs' profits pretty much the same way the Internal Revenue Service does. For example, LLCs do not pay state income taxes, but their members do via their personal tax returns. However, there are some exemptions. a few of them charge LLCs taxes on the income they make on top of the income tax their members have to pay on the same income. An example of this is the state of California, which imposes an income tax on LLCs that earn more than $250,000 annually. These income taxes can go as high as $9000.

It is not a tax on their income; other states charge LLCs annual fees such as franchise taxes, renewal fees, or annual registrations. Among such states are Delaware, California, Massachusetts, Illinois, New Hampshire, Wyoming, and Pennsylvania. Most charge only about $100 annually except for California, Illinois, Massachusetts, and Pennsylvania, which charge $800, $300, $500, and $330, respectively, every year.

If you consider these as significant tax considerations, inquire with your state's tax or revenue Department before forming an LLC. in matters like these, you have to ensure all bases are covered.

The Effect of Corporate Taxation on LLC Taxes

Whether an LLC can be tax-beneficial for you depends on what you plan to do with the profits regularly. If you plan to keep most or all of its income in the business for future expansion, then electing for corporate taxation as an LLC will be good for you. If you want your LLC to be tax like a corporation, i.e., a flat corporate tax rate, you can elect to do so by filing IRS Form 8832 and check the box on the form, which indicates "corporate treatment." After electing for this tax treatment, the profits you leave in the company will be taxed using the corporate tax rate, and you, as an owner, need not pay personal income taxes on them.

Depending on the average annual income of your LLC, corporate tax rates may lead to lower taxes. This is because corporate tax rates are flat, while personal income tax rates increase as the income also increases. To get a clear picture of the most likely tax scenario, you should check with a professional tax accountant if you elect corporate taxation. This is especially because doing so locks it up as a corporate taxpayer for the next five taxable years. You cannot go back to pass-through taxation if you regret the change within the said time frame. And even if you decide to do so after the five years are over, you and your business may experience tax consequences. Again, the importance of thinking very carefully about electing for corporate taxation cannot be overemphasized.

Chapter 8: S Corporations

An S corporation combines liability protection for its owners and passes through Federal income taxation. It is a variation of a regular corporation that can be found under subchapter S of Chapter 1 of the IRC.

If you want your business to be classified as an S Corporation, the first step is to register it as a regular corporation. To do this, you must file and submit certain kinds of documents such as a certificate of incorporation and articles of incorporation with the SEC or any government agency. You will also need to pay the fees required by the institutions.

After you've successfully incorporated your business, you and all other stockholders need to submit a signed Form 2553 to acquire an S Corp designation. after your business has successfully been tax identified as an S Corp, income taxes will then be filed and paid individually by you and all other owners on your personal returns.

According to the Internal Revenue Service, your Corporation needs to meet these requirements to qualify:

- It must be based or domiciled in the United States

- It must have only allowable stockholders, which may include individuals, estates, and specific types of trusts and must exclude non-resident alien stockholders, and business entities such as partnerships and corporations

- The number of stockholders must not exceed 100

- The company must have only one classification of stock

- It must not be a disqualified corporation under the S Corp structure, e.g., specific types of financial institutions, domestic, international sales corporations, and insurance companies.

Double Taxation: How to Avoid It

To avoid being taxed twice on the same income, it is important two no, what the IRS says about an S Corp regarding federal income taxation.

"Generally, an S corporation is exempt from federal income tax other than tax on certain capital gains and passive income. It is treated in the same way as a partnership, in that generally; taxes are not paid at the corporate level."

Of all its features, many investors consider this one of the most desirable. It is because a regular corporation's taxable income is subject to double taxation. The first taxation is at the corporate level, while the second one is at the personal level via the stockholders' dividend income taxes.

In the example we looked at earlier in the chapter on LLCs, you saw how double taxation on a regular corporation looks like. If your Corporation elects to be an S Corp, its pass-through income taxation scheme practically eliminates double taxation. Because the corporation's profits and losses are reported in their shareholders' individual tax returns, an S Corp need not pay income taxes.

However, not all S Corps are given this privilege. Some states and municipalities have passed laws that deny these business entities such benefits.

Take, for example, New York City. The city levies a full corporate income tax of 8.85% on S Corps. But if the Corporation can establish it has businesses outside of New York, then the income attributable to them can be exempted from this flat rate. Similarly, California imposes a franchise tax of 1.5% of an S Corp's annual net income or at least $800, whichever is higher.

If you choose an S Corp, you will use Form 1120S to file its income tax return. As with LLCs, profits, losses, and deductions of shareholders are itemized under schedule K-1.

Considerations for Choosing an S Corp Structure

Before deciding whether to elect for taxed as an S Corp, consider its advantages and disadvantages in relation to your preferences, needs, and objectives.

S Corp Advantages

One benefit associated with electing to become an S Corp is lower self-employment taxes. Under this taxable entity status, there are two components, which are salary and distribution. As an S Corp, only one component triggers the self-employment tax: salary. You can reduce your overall tax liability through lower self-employment taxes.

Contrast this with other types of business entities like sole props, partnerships, and limited liability corporations. With these businesses, Self-employment taxes are triggered by the entire net income of the business. So, you will need to pay self-employment taxes based on the entire profits regardless if you keep the profits in the business or not.

The second component which is distributions to shareholders or owners, aren't taxed. Because an S Corp can make a reasonable distinction between the salary and distribution components of income, it can give you a significant amount of tax savings. If you're inclined to use this division to minimize your taxes, a good rule of thumb is to withdraw around 60% of your business is net income as salary because otherwise, it may trigger the IRS to look into your business for potential tax avoidance.

Another benefit associated with this type of business entity is an independent life. What does this mean?

With other kinds of businesses, their going concern is tied to their owners' mortality or exit from the business. But this isn't the case with an S Corp, whose survival is independent of its owners. Regardless if owners stay, depart, or die, it will continue to live. This type of independence makes it an ideal business structure if you're looking at long term growth and longevity.

The third benefit associated with an S Corp is liability protection. Except in certain cases, you will never be personally reliable for your business's debts. Other types of business entities do not prevent their creditors or claimants from coming after your personal assets when it goes bankrupt.

The fourth advantage concerns ownership transfer. Unlike other business entities, it'll be much easier for you to transfer your ownership later on, should you get out of the business. There are two ways you can do this.

The first one is through an outright sale of your stake in the business, where in exchange for monetary considerations, ownership is immediately transferred to the buyer. The second way you can transfer ownership is through a gradual sale. Under this option, selling your stake in the business takes place over a specific time frame. You may think of it as akin to an installment or amortization scheme. Regardless of which option is taken, you must formalize the entire ownership transfer process via printed and signed sales agreement.

The final advantage of electing to be an S Corp is credibility. Because This business entity is recognized among many prospective investors, customers, and vendors, electing as an S Corp may give your business more credibility in the market.

Possible Disadvantages

While there are numerous advantages your business can enjoy when it elects to be an S Corp, it's not without its fair share of disadvantages. One of them is the need to follow many protocols. These include scheduled meetings of stockholders and directors, recording minutes for every meeting, proper records keeping, creating by-laws, and many other kinds of required paperwork.

The second possible disadvantage relates to compensation requirements. S Corp shareholders need to divide corporate income into two components, i.e., salary and distribution. Because these components can be manipulated to maximize that savings or avoid certain taxes, the IRS is stricter about suspicious combinations of these two components like a low salary but high distributions. If you are guilty of setting a low salary but giving a huge amount in terms of income distribution, the IRS can force certain changes. This includes increasing the salary portion and reducing the distributions component for tax reporting purposes. When this happens, you can expect a bigger tax bill.

Another potential issue related to this business entity is added cost and work. Compared to other structures such as a sole proprietorship, your business will require more accounting and bookkeeping work. This means you will need to hire a qualified accountant and bookkeeper to ensure your financial records are in order. This can lead to higher expenses. Besides that, it may also need more professional advice from bankers and lawyers to address other business areas, such as obtaining financing, filing of taxes, and others. Requiring more professional services can push your expense envelope even higher.

And depending on the state or locality your S Corp will be located; it may also pay more taxes by way of fees and other charges. Massachusetts, for example, charges more taxes on profits after exceeding a specific amount.

Going for an S Corp, we also placed added restrictions on your business. The IRS has put in place several restrictions for businesses to qualify as S Corps. These include restrictions on the number and the shareholders allowed. Some of these include:

- Foreign individuals cannot be stockholders

- Stockholders need to be either permanent residents or United States citizens

- Transfer of ownership can be done only to specifically identified individuals, trusts, and estates

If a business violates regulations like these, the chances are high that the Internal Revenue Service will revoke the entity's S Corp status. Compliance with many restrictions is a must, and it can make the business much less flexible compared to others.

It's also worth noting that the company's income and losses have to be distributed to its shareholders according to their ownership percentage. Unlike partnerships or limited liability corporations, your business is not free to use other income distribution methods.

As a small business, you may benefit much from being an S Corp., but if yours is a big, fast, and growing one, maybe a regular or C corporation status might be better for you. This is because it can issue many kinds of stocks with a virtually unlimited number of shareholders and practically no restrictions on who can own shares.

Finally, future tax changes have the potential to impact you negatively as a taxpayer if you choose an S Corp status. Take, for example, what happened in 2013 when the IRS height the top rate for individual taxpayers from 35% to 39.6%. If you are a single-filing individual burning more than $400,000 or a joint-filing one earning a combined income of over $450,000, Your tax bracket is now higher than the corporate tax rate.

Developments like these highlight the importance of being up-to-date with tax regulations. Otherwise, you may fail to take advantage of tax benefits or, worse, pay more taxes.

Should You, or Shouldn't You?

Because of its tax savings and investor protection characteristics, many American companies elect for S Corp status. it also helps that compared to some other forms of business entities, this type has an advantage in terms of transferring ownership and business continuity.

But if you are the sole owner in your business is small, i.e., making less than $50,000 every year, this setup may be more disadvantageous than beneficial. That is why before electing to be an S Corp, make sure you have extensively researched governing rules and regulations at the federal, state, and even local government levels. And if you want to make sure it would be wise for you to hire a lawyer specializing in corporate structures and taxes.

How S Corporations are Taxed

The IRS considers an S Corp as a mere pass-through entity for taxation purposes. This means taxes on its income are ultimately passed down to its owners for purposes of paying income taxes. Except for this, this kind of business entity operates pretty much the same as regular corporations.

If your business elects for this tax status, this is how you file federal income taxes:

- The company uses Form 1120-S to file its corporate tax return

- It records every shareholder's allocation of income or loss using Schedule K-1

- You and other shareholders report K-1 information on line 17 of Form 1040

For state tax determination, many use federal information on taxpayers' total income. Hence, it is very important to get the filing and payment of federal income taxes right.

As an owner of an S Corp, you pay income taxes based on your distributive share of the company's net income. If yours is a single LLC elected to be one, then the entire net income is yours. You will use Form 1040 to report these taxes.

One of the most lamented concerns related to a regular corporation is double taxation. While the law prohibits double taxation of individuals, the double taxation that happens with regular corporations' income is one that applies to two different parties. But with an S Corp, this is not an issue. By being a mere pass-through entity for tax purposes, its income is taxed as its owners' personal income. Unlike regular corporations taxed at the corporate level and later at the personal income level because of dividends, income from an S Corp is only taxed once.

Self-Employment Taxes

Shareholders of a regular corporation get returns on their investments via dividends. But owners of an S Corp be regular income taxes on their share of the company's income, but the IRS does not consider them as self-employed. Thus, you won't have to pay self-employment taxes on your share of the company's income. But if you are also an employee of the company and receive a salary from it, you will need to pay FICA or self-employment taxes such as Social Security and Medicare. Thus, owner-employees of an S Corp are subject to this tax.

Other S Corp Taxes

Just like other businesses, your S Corp will also pay other business taxes. These include employment or payroll taxes, the state-imposed excise and sales taxes, and state-specific taxes on S Corps such as gross receipts, franchise, and income taxes.

S Corporations Vs. LLCs

After reading the characteristics, benefits, and disadvantages you may be thinking, what makes it different from a limited liability corporation? One of the ways they differ from each other is taxes.

Unlike a limited liability corporation, an S Corp is not considered a formal business entity. Instead, an S Corp is more of an elected method for determining your business's tax status or how it will be taxed. As a tax status, it avoids being taxed twice, i.e., at the corporate and personal levels via the business's net income and dividends, respectively.

Interestingly, your limited liability corporation can elect to be taxed as an S Corp or a C Corp. To help you decide which one, remember that state laws govern an LLC while an S or C Corp is governed by federal tax laws through the IRS.

Still speaking of taxes, you need to pay self-employment taxes as an owner or member of an LLC. These include Medicare and Social Security taxes you will pay directly to the Internal Revenue Service. As of 2020, 12.4% is the self-employment income tax rate for Social Security, while it's only 2.9% for Medicare. Remember that to compute self-employment taxes as an LLC member, the company's entire net income is taxable.

But with an S Corp, you are given a salary as a shareholder, and the business pays your payroll taxes. The company can claim your salary as legitimate business expenses to reduce its taxable income. If it registers residual income after all deductions are made, these are distributed to you and other members as dividends and are taxed at a lower rate compared to regular income.

Another way that the two differ from each other is in terms of management structure. A single-member LLC is run like a sole proprietorship, while a multiple-member LLC is like a partnership when the members themselves manage the business. But if they hire professional managers to run it, the structure more closely resembles that of a corporation. Being hands-off in its daily activities, they will only provide corporate direction and oversight like a corporation's board of directors do. But with S corporations, they usually have officers and directors oversee the business, make major decisions, and delegate managers to run the business.

Finally, S corporations differ from LLC's in terms of ownership. For one, your business cannot have over 100 shareholders as an S Corp, but as an LLC, it can have as many members as you want.

Another ownership related difference is that your S Corp isn't allowed to have shareholders that are not US citizens. But if it's an LLC, you can accommodate members that are neither residents nor Americans.

Another ownership related difference involves subsidiaries. As an S Corporation, you cannot own or set up any, but as an LLC, you can do so with no restrictions.

The final ownership difference between these two entities involves shares of stock. Choosing an S Corp means your business can issue shares of stock, albeit only one kind. Choosing an LLC, however, you're not allowed to issue any.

Chapter 9: C Corporations

Now that we're done discussing a special type of corporation, let's talk about the regular kind: C corporations. These refer to corporations where the company and its owners are taxed separately. This is the most common type of corporation in the United States, and it is subject to corporate income taxes, unlike the other types of businesses. Because the business and its owners are taxed on their income from its business activities, C corporations' income is effectively double-taxed.

This kind of business entity is comparable with S corporations and LLCs because of their ability to protect their owners' assets from creditors and other claimants, especially during bankruptcy. However, it differs from these in terms of tax treatment and legal structures.

Corporations pay taxes on their corporate income, and when they distribute these as dividends to their shareholders, they get taxed as well because it's now considered as their personal income. While income from this business entity is taxed twice, it still gives benefit. First, if the Corporation retains its earnings instead of distributing them as dividends, shareholders like you will not be taxed. Hence, double taxation is avoided.

But the more important benefit pertains to lower tax rates. As of 2020, the top tax rate bracket for individuals is at 37%. This is for single-filing individuals earning over $518,400 annually and for married, joint-filing taxpayers with annual incomes exceeding $622,050. For corporations, the flat income tax rate is 35% only. Think about it; if you're an individual earning this much money every year, you're paying a higher tax rate compared to corporations. This also gives you the benefit of reinvesting your profits back to the company at a lower corporate tax rate.

As a regular or a C Corporation, it needs to require at least one meeting every year attended by stockholders and directors. It will also need to record minutes of such meetings to ensure transparency in its operations. It is also required to maintain voting records for its directors, and accurate records of each shareholder's percentage holdings in the company. Other responsibilities include:

> • Keeping its company by-laws within its primary business premises

> • Filing of annual and financial disclosure reports with a regulatory authority such as the securities and exchange commission (SEC) and the IRS

> • Preparing and submitting financial statements with pertinent government institutions

Should You or Shouldn't You Choose a C Corporation?

To choose carefully, consider these benefits and disadvantages.

C Corporation Benefits

As with the case of an LLC and S Corporation, a C Corporation protects personal assets. The business's creditors and other claimants cannot go after your bank accounts and other financial assets. Your business's legal obligations will never be your own under this setup.

Another benefit is continuity. Even if you or other shareholders die, the business's going concerned will not be impeded, and it will continue to exist and operate. Even if there is a legal battle for who will be the rightful heirs to your or other stockholders' shares in the company absent a will, it will be business as usual for the corporation.

Compared to an S Corp, this business entity can issue more than one type of shares. It can issue common, preferred, and hybrid shares of stock if it does so. It can also accommodate as many shareholders as it once provided it has permission from regulatory authorities such as the SEC. And while it has a ceiling on the number of shares and the amount of authorized capital stock it can accept, it can apply for increases in both, and once approved by the Securities and Exchange Commission; it can proceed. This provides you with practically unlimited access to capital from other investors and yourself For financing future growth and expansion of business activities.

Another key benefit of adopting a C corporation structure is potential tax savings. Many years ago, many tax experts recommended small businesses and startups to register as limited liability companies or LLCs. Before 2013, the top individual income tax rate was practically the same as the flat corporate tax rate. But when the federal government hiked it to almost 40% that year, things changed. The top individual tax rate suddenly became significantly higher than the flat corporate tax rate. Particularly for individuals who make a lot of money via LLCs, paying taxes based on individual tax rates suddenly became irrational.

Even after the Trump administration reduced individual income taxes such that the top read was only 37% in 2017, the corporate flat rate was also cut down from 35% to only 21%. Because LLCs and S corporations pass on tax payments to their individual owners at the individual rate, members and shareholders whose earnings or at the top of the individual tax bracket system be more in taxes compared to C corporations. This has made this type of business entity a popular option for many business owners regardless of the size.

Another important benefit related to C corporations that make it a very popular option for business owners these days is IRC 1202. If you qualify for this, you have a chance to exclude capital gains on investments of up to $10,000,000 or up to ten times the value of your original investment in the C corporation. one of the primary requirements to qualify for IRC 1202 is that you hold your stock investment in the company for at least five years. For more information, check with your professional tax expert.

To summarize, choosing a C corporation for your business may be very advantageous for you if you start a small business, plan to retain most if not all of its income to fund its growth over the years, and cash out after over five years.

How C Corporations are Taxed

Regular or C corporations paid taxes at the corporate level first. Then, when they distribute their post-tax income to its shareholders by way of dividends, the distributions will be taxed on a personal level for the stockholders. This is why, technically, corporations are double-taxed.

While double taxation is a serious concern, it may be mitigated or even avoided. How?

Be aware that these entities are taxed on their net income at the corporate level and not on their revenues. If the Corporation made $10,000,000 in annual sales, operating expenses and costs of goods sold would be deducted from the revenues to determine its net taxable income.

Let's say that cost of goods sold plus operating expenses totaled $7,000,000 for the year. The ducting the amount from its annual revenues, it would be left with a net operating income of $3,000,000. It is this amount that will be subject to income taxes.

Given a flat corporate income tax rate of 26.5%, this company will pay $795,000 in income taxes for the taxable year. As a result, its net income after taxes will be $2,205,000, from which dividends may be distributed to shareholders.

If the company distributes its entire net income for the year as dividends to stockholders. It will again be subjected to another round of income taxation, which will be reported in the shareholders' individual tax returns. But if the company retains all of its earnings for that year to fund future projects and expansion efforts, no dividends will be distributed. Shareholders need not be income taxes on those earnings and avoid double taxation.

Sometimes, double taxation may not be avoided. However, it can be minimized. How?

As a shareholder, you may also be designated as an owner-employee. You may have a regular salary. This salary is beneficial in two ways.

First, it may be claimed as a legitimate business expense and, therefore, can reduce the corporation's taxable income. Second, even if you have to pay personal income taxes on that salary, you can structure it so the applicable personal tax rate may even be lower than the corporate one. So, you not only avoided double taxation for a significant portion of your share of the income, but you also even have a chance of paying a lower rate than the corporate one if you agree on the right amount.

Getting a regular salary from your Corporation isn't the only way to minimize or avoid double taxation. You may also do so through fringe benefits such as dependent care, medical benefits, and life insurance. These are non-taxable benefits on your end and the side of the Corporation; these are deductible expenses. You may not necessarily get your share of the income in money terms, but at least you can use them in non-monetary ways that benefit you and your family.

C corporations must fill out and file IRS Form 1120, which informs the Internal Revenue Service of its income, capital gains, deductions, losses, tax credits and income tax liabilities.

Going back to the issue of double taxation, this is one of the biggest reasons why many businesspeople elect their corporations as an S Corp, assuming all requirements are met. Remember, when a Corporation elects for this tax status, it can pass taxes on its income to its shareholders. Being a pass-through entity, if no longer has to pay corporate income taxes, but instead, its shareholders or owners pay income taxes on their respective shares of the income.

Chapter 10: Sole Proprietorship and Partnerships

Finally, we have come to the last two common business entities in the United States for taxation purposes: sole proprietorships and partnerships. Let's start with sole proprietorships first.

Sole Proprietorships

This type of business has only one owner, and many entrepreneurs use this structure. This is also a business that people operate without setting up an official structure with the state, i.e., default structure.

Is a sole proprietorship business the ideal structure for you? Some indicators it may be are:

• You want the simplest business structure as possible

• You're not concerned with keeping your personal and business assets and liabilities separate

• Your annual profits as an entrepreneur are low to moderate

• You're a neophyte entrepreneur and are still undecided whether going into business is your destiny

How Sole Proprietorships are Taxed

In a sole proprietorship, you and your business are one, i.e., you report all of its business income and losses in your personal income tax returns. Hence, you need not file a separate tax return for it.

When filing tax returns, you must report its profits and losses on Schedule C with your Form 1040. You'll have to pay taxes on the entire income from your sole proprietorship business, even if you retain all of it under the business's bank account.

If you have not filed taxes as a solopreneur, know you must also pay self-employment taxes like social security and Medicare contributions on your own. You may go to the IRS website for the current self-employment tax rate and income ceilings.

Filing your income taxes as a sole proprietor is hardly any different from doing so was an employee. The only key difference is instead of reporting your salaries or wages you receive from your job; you report your business is net income or loss on Schedule C, which is the IRS' form for reporting profits or losses from a business. You will then submit this with form 1040.

You will be taxed on all of your business's profits. However, you must remember that profits differ from wages and salaries because profits are the remaining portion of your revenues after deducting legitimate business expenses. For example, your business registered total sales amounting to $100,000 in the last tax year, while total operating expenses, including the cost of the inventories you sold, amounted to $70,000. You will only pay income taxes on the difference, which is your $30,000 profit.

Contrast this to your salaries or wages as an employee. Assuming your total salaries and wages during the last taxable year amounted to $100,000, too. You will be paying income taxes, which your employer would have withheld, on the entire $100,000. So, this is practically the key difference between filing income taxes as a sole proprietor and as a worker or employee earning wages.

Though your sole proprietorship business and you are the same, apply the business entity accounting principle. If you have forgotten, it is the practice of keeping financial records, assets, and liabilities off your business separate from your personal ones. By doing so, you avoid reporting wrong amounts for income, losses, financial assets, and liabilities. You also avoid risks of mismanaging your business due to the comingling of your personal and business accounts.

Another key tax difference between operating a sole proprietorship and being an employee involves computing and filing taxes. As an employee, your employer is responsible for estimating, deducting, depositing, and filing your income taxes related to the wages, you receive from him or her. But as a sole proprietor, you will be responsible for all things related to your income taxes, including estimating, payment, and filing with the pertinent tax authorities.

As a sole proprietor, you will also need to pay self-employment or FICA taxes, including Medicare and Social Security. As a single business owner, this is the equivalent of payroll taxes for employees. But compared to being an employee, you are a higher amount because, as both owner and employee of your business, you are responsible for the contributions of the employer and the employee. Also, you don't have the benefit of somebody computing and withholding your contributions for you.

As of 2020, the self-employment tax rate is 15.3%. This is broken down into Medicare and Social Security, With 2.9% and 12.4%, respectively.

Partnerships

A partnership is owned and operated by more than one person or business entity. You and other people can form one through an informal agreement or a written one. However, it's best to have your agreement properly documented so it will be easy to clarify and resolve issues should they arise.

Partnerships are similar to sole proprietorships because they don't pay income taxes, but instead, they pass it on to their owners. Another similarity between the two is that partnerships and their owners are considered the same. This means their financial liabilities are obligations of their owners, too. Creditors and other parties with claims on the business can go after the personal assets of its owners. So, if you choose a partnership business, you must keep this lack of protection in mind.

But compared to a sole proprietorship, a partnership gives you the advantage of additional capital. You don't have to bear all the capitalization responsibilities alone because you can count on your partners; it also contributes their capital share.

Additional capitalization isn't the only way you can benefit from having partners in your business. More heads mean more expertise, skills, experience, and labor for the business. As with capitalization, you don't have to bear the burdens of managing and growing the business alone.

However, you will need to be very careful about the partners you will choose. You need to be certain that they are people you can trust both in terms of skill and integrity. We should also choose partners with similar or the same visions and values for the business. Doing so can minimize the risks for frequent disagreements, partner conflicts, and fraud.

If you set up a partnership for a business, you can choose from four types:

- General partnerships
- Limited liability company (LLC) partnerships
- Limited liability partnerships
- Limited partnerships

General Partnership

This is the most basic partnership. You can farm this with other people or businesses, and you don't have to establish or register it with your state formally. That is why of all the types come on, this is the easiest one you can establish with partners.

A general partnership can give you relative flexibility with taxes. However, not only does it not offer liability protection, but it also means you and your partners are jointly and severally liable for the business. This means if one of your partners puts the business at risk resulting in claims by other parties, your personal assets may be at risk. That is why I can never overemphasize the importance of choosing the right partners.

Limited Liability Company (LLC) Partnership

As its name suggests, you and your partners enjoy the benefit of personal liability protection, just like an LLC. Also called a *multi-member limited liability Corporation*, this partnership also offers relative tax flexibility, but you, as a member, may be held accountable for the actions of your other co-members or partners.

Limited Liability Partnership

This one is formally established and agreed upon by you and your partners compared to a general partnership. And compared to an LLC partnership, this business gives you protection against claims arising from both your partners' actions and the business's liabilities. However, protection against personal liability for claims against the business doesn't extend to those arising from your personal negligence, malicious intent, or malpractice.

Limited liability partnerships give you flexibility in terms of managing the business, but unlike the first two types, they do not provide tax flexibility. And in some states, establishing LLPs is an option that is available only to certain types of professions. That is why it's important to check with your state if the LLP you plan to set up with other people is qualified.

Limited Partnership

There are two types of partners under a limited partnership: a general partner and a limited one. Under the law, limited partnerships need to have at least one general partner.

The general partner exercises a great deal of control over the business's operations and decisions. He or she is personally responsible for the business, i.e., personally liable. If there are no general partners, nobody would be responsible for the business. That is why the government requires that at least one partner is general.

But the limited partner is not involved in making decisions for and running the business. Also known as a silent partner, he or she is not personally liable for the business; hence, the designation or title. When it comes to tax flexibility, you may enjoy some with this type of partnership.

How Partnerships Are Taxed

Because partnerships do not pay income taxes while its owners do on their personal returns, they are considered as merely pass-through entities. As a result, the partner with the biggest ownership share of the business pays higher taxes on the business income than the others.

As a partner, you will file your share of the business's income with the IRS using Form 1065. You and your partners will get a copy of Schedule K, a document that identifies you and your other partners' share of the business's income and expenses. You will attach this form upon filing your personal tax returns.

Should You Choose a Partnership?

To answer this question, you must weigh its pros and cons relative to your and your partners' preferences and goals. Let's take a look at the benefits first.

Partnership Pros

Compared to a single proprietorship, a partnership gives you more of everything good. You have access to greater funding, extra hands on deck for managing the business, and synergistic combinations of business skills, experiences, and networks. Two heads, bank accounts, and management skills are better than one.

Another benefit of choosing a partnership over other types of businesses, such as a corporation, is taxation. Because it is a pass-through entity, i.e., the business is income taxes are passed on to you and the other owners, double taxation is avoided. If you recall, see corporations or regular corporations are taxed twice, first at the corporate level and then at the personal or stockholders' level.

Potential Partnership Cons

One of the possible disadvantages of choosing this type of business over a sole proprietorship is sharing control over the business with other people. This is especially true if you're the type of person who likes to be in complete control over the business and doesn't like sharing responsibilities with others. If you're a person who's also averse to conflicts, this may not be the business model for you.

Another potential issue with this type of business may be the lack of a formal structure or agreement. As mentioned earlier, you can form a partnership with other people, even with a verbal agreement. But this arrangement can prove problematic when conflicts arise because there is no objective basis for settling them. You may say you agreed upon this, while the other partners may claim otherwise.

Fortunately, this can be easily remedied. Just make sure to document your partnership agreement formally with every member or partner signing it. That way, you have something objective to refer to when there are disagreements or conflicts.

Also, if you want to keep all the profits to yourself, this is obviously impossible with a partnership. At the very least, you will need to share its income proportionately according to each partner's capital or industrial contributions.

Finally, this business exposes you to the risks of being liable for your partners' actions. Forming a general or an LLC partnership makes you accountable for the consequences of your partner's negligence, malfeasance, or malpractice.

Chapter 11: Self-Employment for Small Businesses

Many people get confused between self-employment and entrepreneurship. If you're one of them, then this chapter is for you.

So, how can you determine if you are a self-employed businessperson? You can start by asking yourself these questions:

- In your business, do you feel like you're working all the time and can't take breaks?

- Do you find it hard to define your specific role in the business accurately, especially if you are responsible for many things?

- Do you take on several roles in your business's operations?

- Will your business grind to a screeching halt if you're not around?

If you've answered "yes" to any of these questions, especially the last one, then you are highly likely to be a self-employed businessperson.

And if you are curious to know what distinguishes a self-employed businessperson from a regular business owner, here it is: as a self-employed individual, you are the business, while as a small business owner, you just run one. That is why a critical component of being a self-employed business owner is that the business will not run without you because you are the business.

Here are other ways to help you determine whether you're really a self-employed entrepreneur or are simply a regular business owner:

- Being self-employed, you are responsible for all aspects of the business while as a business owner, you delegate most tasks to other people

- If you work in the business alone, you are self-employed while if you employ people, you are a business owner

- If you are working part-time on the business, are working even after retiring or have W2 income, you're self-employed

- If your business has minimal start-up and overhead costs, you're probably self-employed

- If your business needs capital to continue and grow, you are a business owner rather than self-employed

Self-Employment Taxes

If you're a self-employed small business owner, then you must pay self-employment taxes. These are the equivalent of payroll taxes if you're an employee rather than a self-employed business owner.

It's tempting to think that if you're a self-employed small business owner who doesn't hire any employees, you don't have to concern yourself with managing payroll taxes. Nothing can be farther from the truth. Even if you don't hire other people to help you run your business, there will always be that one person working for your business: you! that is why you're called self-employed, right? You are still technically responsible for "payroll taxes."

As a self-employed entrepreneur, you do not have to withhold taxes on your business's income you withdraw. In its stead, however, you may need to pay estimated income taxes every quarter. And if you earn over $400 annually from your business, you must pay self-employment taxes.

As a self-employed entrepreneur, self-employment taxes (SECA) are the equivalent of the employer-employee based FICA taxes. If you are operating a sole proprietorship, a partnership, or a limited liability company, you pay self-employment taxes based on your self-employment net income. In simpler terms, it is based on your share of the business's net income, i.e., revenues fewer expenses.

Similar to FICA taxes, your SECA taxes can also be broken down into Medicare and Social Security. The minimum rate is 15.3% of your total share of the business is net income with Social Security taking 12.4% and Medicare accounting for 2.9%. What makes it different this time is as a self-employed individual, you are responsible for the employer and the employee's contributions. Hence, your self-employment taxes are higher compared to payroll taxes as an employee.

For tax years 2013 and beyond, an additional 0.9% surcharge tax is imposed for the Medicare portion for self-employment income that exceeds specific threshold amounts. For married individuals filing jointly with their spouses, the combined threshold is $250,000, while for those who are married but file separately from their spouses, the individual threshold is $125,000. For all other tax filing statuses, the threshold is $200,000.

Allowed Tax Deductions for Small, Self-Employed Business

Whether it's income tax or self-employment taxes, always remember that the base amount is the business's net income and not revenues. This means that your taxable income as a self-employed individual is already net of certain allowable expense deductions.

What are the allowable deductions you can make for tax purposes? Besides self-employment taxes, these include the following.

Home Office Expenses

You may claim any expense you incur in relation to regular and exclusive use of any space in your home for your small business's operations as a home expense deduction regardless if you own or rent it. One interesting aspect of the deduction is while it is based on the honor system, i.e., honesty system, you will need to defend your computations well if the IRS audits your business. Here, you must be creative in how you can objectively establish the basis for your home office expense computations and claims.

One of the best ways you can justify these claims is by creating a diagram of your office space, which clearly identifies that portion of your home used for such purposes and its exact measurements. This is because home office expense tax deductions are largely based on your home's area and the exact portion used exclusively and regularly for your small business's operations. With a diagram that provides accurate and detailed information you should have an easy time defending your position.

Aside from the area of your home dedicated to running your small business, you may also claim other expenses. These include:

- Depreciation expenses of the home
- Home repair and maintenance expenses paid during the taxable year

- Homeowners insurance
- Interest on the home mortgage
- Property or real estate taxes paid
- Utility expenses

The same rule applies for determining the amount. That you can claim on the above-mentioned expenses, for example, if your Home Office takes up 20% of the total floor area of your home, it means you may only claim up to 20% of the number of expenses. Let's say your home's utility bills amounted to $2000. This means you can only claim up to 20% or $400 as a tax-deductible home expense for your small business.

It's also worth noting that you can only claim for some of these expenses if you own your home. These include interest on a mortgage, homeowners' insurance, and home depreciation.

You can choose from two calculation methods to determine your home office deductions: the standard and simplified methods. When you choose one, you aren't restricted to using the same method every year.

Should you choose the standard method, you will need to determine the actual amount you paid for your home office expenses. So, this can be a bit tedious.

If you go with the simplified version, you will just multiply the actual area of your home office space with the pre-determined rate from the Internal Revenue Service. You may not claim depreciation and other itemized home-related deductions under this method. You can also only use the simplified version if your home office space's floor area is 300 square feet at most.

Which is better? That would depend on your situation and your preferences. If you're a very busy person and/or aren't able to maintain accurate records of all of your tax-deductible home office expenses, then going for the simplified version is the better option for you. However, the standard method may be the optimal choice if you:

- Use over 300 square feet of Home Office space

- Spend a lot of money on utilities

- You can maintain excellent records of all home-related expenses

But if you want to make sure which of the two methods will give you optimal tax deductions, use both methods to estimate you're allowed tax deductions given your home office space's area, the percentage of total home floor area it occupies, and actual expenses. Use IRS Form 8829 - Expenses for Business Use of Your Home - to calculate your home expense deductions based on the standard method.

Communications Bills

These include the use of a landline phone, fax, and the Internet. Just remember that you can only deduct the portion of these expenses used directly for your small business. For example, if you have only one landline phone in your home, it's obviously used for personal and office use. This means you cannot deduct the entire bill on the income tax return but only the portion directly attributable to business use, which may be challenging to prove. But if you have two landline phones and one is used exclusively for business, then you can claim the entire cost for that line as deductions.

The same goes for your Internet-related expenses. You can only claim deductions in proportion to the time you used it for the business unless you subscribed to two accounts, and one of them is exclusively for the business.

Health Insurance

If you're a married, self-employed business owner, you weren't qualified to be included in your employed spouse's health insurance plan, and you pay for your own health insurance premiums, you are eligible to clean your entire health, dental, and qualified long-term care insurance premiums. And whether or not they are your declared dependents, you may also claim as deductions health insurance premiums paid to cover your spouse and children below 27 years old by the end of the taxable year. You may use IRS Publication 535's Self-Employed Health Insurance Deduction Worksheet to compute for your health insurance premium deductions.

Meals

These are tax-deductible Expenses you incur during business-related travels and entertainment expenses. You may only claim up to 50% of the meal's actual cost as deductions if you have the official receipt, but if you don't, you may still do so, provided you keep records of the business purpose, time, and please for the travel. And if you think that the lunch you eat at your office desk is tax-deductible, sorry to burst your bubble, but it isn't.

Travel Expenses

You may claim all travel-related expenses provided that the business trip lasts more than an ordinary business day, must take place outside of your tax home's general area (out of the city or state), and it must require you to rest or sleep in between.

For your travel to count as an official business trip, you must have a particular business purpose before leaving your home, and you must or form actual business activities like looking for new prospects and customers, doing client call visits, attending workshops or classes that will help you increase your skills directly related to the business you're operating. And no, going to a bar in another state to celebrate your cousin's promotion and handing out business cards during the event doesn't count as a tax-deductible travel expense.

Always keep accurate and complete records, especially official receipts, to support all of your business travel expenses and activities. Travel expenses are one of the most noticed types by the IRS, and if you claim them without adequate documentary support, you may get into trouble.

To help you avoid any wrong claims, here are some of the most common deductible travel expenses:

- Airplane fare

- Cost of land transportation to your destination like Uber, subway and bus tickets, or car rentals

- Board and lodging

- Meals

Always remember that extravagant or lavish expenses are not tax-deductible. However, it doesn't mean you always have to choose the cheapest and crappiest options. The key here is reasonable. The IRS puts a limit on the amount spent on travel-related expenses because at the end of the day, American taxpayers will carry the bulk of the cost. Americans bear every dollar of tax deductions, hence, the need to keep expenses like these to reasonable amounts.

Except for your meals, all travel-related expenses can be 100% deductible. You may only claim up to 50% of your travel-related meal expenses.

But what if you be more efficient by scheduling pleasure and business-related activities in one trip? Then, be prepared for or more complicated claiming process. This is because you can only claim the portion of such trips related directly to your business as deductions. This means you must find an objective way to determine how much of your trip is for business and pleasure.

Vehicle Expenses

Whenever you use your personal vehicle to run your business, those trips are eligible for tax deductions. To take advantage of this benefit, keep accurate records of information for claiming them in your tax returns, such as:

- Date of the trips

- Trip mileages

- The business purpose for each trip

Remember, you may not claim personal trips as official ones for purposes of claiming tax deductions.

You have two options for computing how much you can claim: actual expenses and the IRS' standard mileage rates. As of 2020, The standard mileage rate for businesses is 57.5 cents per mile. The standard mileage rate is the more convenient option because both record-keeping and the calculation processes are minimal. You need only to record the actual mileage for each trip and their dates. Then, simply sum up the miles for the period and multiply the amount by the standard mileage rate to arrive at your deductible vehicle expenses.

If you choose the actual expense method, be prepared for a more complicated process. First, you must record both the business-related miles and total miles to determine the percentage of your business miles to the total. Next, you must record all expenses related to using your vehicle accurately, including those for gasoline, maintenance, and repairs. Remember that you will need to keep supporting documents such as official receipts and invoices. Finally, you multiply the percentage obtained in the first step by the total expenses.

Let's say your car registered a total of 1000 miles during the tax year, and based on your records, 400 of them were for business-related trips. The business's percentage of total mileage is then 40%. If your total vehicle-related expenses amounted to $1000, multiplying it by 40% gives you a tax-deductible amount of $400.

So, which of the two should you use? You may use the same criteria for home office deductions for deciding.

Rentals

This doesn't just pertain to rented office space. You can also deduct the amount you paid for renting equipment, and if you need to pay a lease termination fee for your business, you may also claim the amount as a deduction. And obviously, you can't claim deductions on rental expenses on properties or equipment you own, even partially.

Startup Expenses

The Internal Revenue Service often compels businesses to amortize the expenses on major acquisitions of capital assets, such as building, equipment, and improvements through annual depreciation. However, it allows certain exceptions. One of them our startup expenses.

When starting a new business, you may deduct up to $5000 of related expenses in your tax returns. Startup expenses include:

- Advertising
- Market research
- Ocular inspections for potential business locations
- Professional fees, including accountant and lawyer fees
- Trave
- State filing and legal fees if the business you're setting up is an LLC or a regular corporation

Remember that purchasing capital assets such as vehicles or equipment do not qualify as startup expenses, and therefore, you can't claim them as such. However, you made appreciate them as capital expenditures over the years through annual depreciation.

Others

While this isn't an exhaustive list, here are other expenses you can claim as deductions being a self-employed small business owner:

- Advertising
- Business insurance premiums such as credit, business liability, and fire insurance
- Cost of continuing education directly related to your line of work or business
- Interest on business loans
- Subscriptions to specialized publications directly related to your business

Self-Employed Business Success Resources

As a self-employed business owner, things can be much more challenging. One reason is being the business itself; you are responsible for most, if not all, of the workload. If the business you're operating is a simple one with few transactions, you're in luck. But what if it's complicated and involves lots of transactions? What should you do?

Well, you have two options. One is you can continue using a DIY approach. However, you may run the risk of spreading yourself too thin, and the quality of your work, and the service and products you provide to your customers may suffer.

The other option involves taking advantage of resources that can help you reduce the burden while improving your business's efficiency and productivity. Here are some of those resources.

Professional Services

If you consider your business's important components, you will find that some of them - though important - do not contribute directly to the bottom line. Worse, they can take up so much of your time and energy. Examples of these are bookkeeping, accounting, and tax management. If your self-employed business deals with many customers and involves voluminous transactions, these can be major productivity and time vampires.

Fortunately, you don't have to take care of these yourself. You can hire professional bookkeepers, accountants, and tax experts to do these things for you. Though it may cost you more money, it can free up more of your time so you can focus more on other aspects of the business that directly contribute to the bottom line. These include sales and marketing.

Another important, albeit non-monetary benefit, is stress reduction. Bookkeeping, accounting, and taxes can be very stressful, especially if you do them wrong, and the authorities discover. By delegating these activities to experts, you can have peace of mind and more time to rest.

Technology

Even if you do the bookkeeping and accounting for your business, you can use technology to make it much easier and more accurate. For example, you can purchase or subscribe to accounting software services. Many of the top developers provide key functions such as receivables management, issuance of invoices, preparation of financial statements, and taxes. You need to do only to input transactions, and the software will take care of everything from organizing information to prepare updated financial statements to accurately totaling numbers.

If you work with lots of freelancers on business projects, you can also use project management tools like Trello and Microsoft To-Do List to coordinate and monitor progress accurately. Programs like these provide many important benefits, such as automatic reminders for both you and your freelancers to ensure timelines are met regularly. These also ensure that neither you nor the people you collaborate with forget what you need to do.

Freelancers

With the advent of the Internet and several job sourcing platforms such as Upwork, it is now easy to find freelancers to complete specific tasks for you and your business. This can be a powerful personal productivity tool for you as a self-employed businessperson.

Let's say you own and run a graphic arts business. Your revenues are limited to the number of hours you can work on clients' projects. Unfortunately, you have the same time as everybody else every day: 24 hours. By tapping high-quality freelance graphic artists, you can take on more projects than you could if you worked alone, effectively scaling up your business.

Hiring freelancers is also a cost-efficient way of scaling up your business because you can pay them on a per-project basis. Compared to hiring a full-time employee for your business, you only pay freelancers when you need to do certain projects. With our graphic art business, you will only book the graphic artist when there are new client projects available. When there's none, you need not hire or pay one. And for optimal business management efficiency and minimal stress, you can simply farm out all projects to your freelancers if your business model allows it.

Conclusion

I hope that within the pages of this book, you have come to understand what tax accounting is, and more important, how to do it properly for your small business.

But for you to benefit from what you've learned, *knowing isn't enough.* As the saying goes, knowing is only half the battle. The other half is the application of knowledge or action. That is why I highly recommend you act on what you've learned soon. It could be as simple as getting more information from your tax accountant or The IRS or changing how you do your business's taxation or changing its structure or entity. Regardless, the important thing is to act on what you've learned immediately. The longer you put it off, the higher the risks of forgetting what you've learned in this book.

Here's another book by Greg Shields that you might like

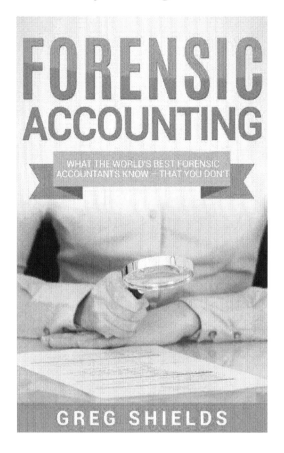

References

Business Partnerships: What You Need to Know - businessnewsdaily.com. (n.d.). Business News Daily. https://www.businessnewsdaily.com/15746-business-partnership-pros-and-cons.html

C Corporation Taxes | How a C Corporation is Taxed | DoMyLLC. (n.d.). DoMyLLC.com. https://www.domyllc.com/c-corp/taxes/

Corporate Taxation: How a C-Corp is Taxed | Rocket Lawyer. (n.d.). Www.Rocketlawyer.com. https://www.rocketlawyer.com/article/c-corp-taxation.rl

Employment Taxes 101: An Owner's Guide to Payroll Taxes. (2020, June 12). Paychex. https://www.paychex.com/articles/payroll-taxes/employers-guide-to-payroll-taxes

FreshBooks. (n.d.). *25 Tax Deductions for a Small Business | What to Expense 2019-2020.* FreshBooks. https://www.freshbooks.com/hub/expenses/tax-deductions-small-business

How Your Business Structure Affects Your U.S. Taxes | FreshBooks Blog. (2017, August 29). FreshBooks Blog - Resources & Advice for Small Business Owners. https://www.freshbooks.com/blog/business-structure-taxes

Internal Revenue Service | An official website of the United States government. (n.d.). https://www.irs.gov/

Investopedia. (2019). *Sharper Insight. Smarter Investing.* Investopedia. https://www.investopedia.com

LLC or S Corporation: What's Better for Your Business? - businessnewsdaily.com. (n.d.). Business News Daily. https://www.businessnewsdaily.com/15339-llc-vs-scorporation.html

Nolo. (2007, December 13). *How Sole Proprietors are Taxed*. Bplans Blog. https://articles.bplans.com/how-sole-proprietors-are-taxed

Operations 1, N. A. I. S. B. (2019, April 30). *Does a C Corporation make sense for my small business?* Small Business Trends. https://smallbiztrends.com/2019/04/c-corporation-small-business.html

SBA. (2019). *Choose a business structure*. Choose a Business Structure. https://www.sba.gov/business-guide/launch-your-business/choose-business-structure

Tax Accounting (Meaning) | Learn Basics of Tax Accounting. (2019, August 26). WallStreetMojo. https://www.wallstreetmojo.com/tax-accounting/

The Role of Tax Accountants. (2012). Chron.com. https://work.chron.com/role-tax-accountants-14140.html

Made in the USA
Las Vegas, NV
30 September 2024

95996158R00072